USDA

United States Department of Agriculture

I0411867

CLIMATE CHANGE EFFECTS
in El Yunque National Forest, Puerto Rico, and the Caribbean Region

Lisa Nicole Jennings, Jamison Douglas, Emrys Treasure, and Grizelle González

Forest Service
Research & Development
Southern Research Station
General Technical Report SRS-193

The Authors:

Lisa Nicole Jennings, Natural Resource Specialist, USDA Forest Service, Grandfather Ranger District, Pisgah National Forest, 109 East Lawing Drive, Nebo, NC 28761; **Jamison Douglas**, Research Associate, North Carolina State University, College of Natural Resources, Department of Forest and Environmental Resources, Campus Box 7260, Raleigh, NC 27695; **Emrys Treasure**, Biological Scientist, USDA Forest Service, Southern Research Station, Eastern Forest Environmental Threat Assessment Center, Raleigh, NC 27606; and **Grizelle González**, Project Leader, USDA Forest Service, International Institute of Tropical Forestry, Jardín Botaníco Sur, Río Piedras, PR 00926.

Cover Photos

TOP ROW LEFT TO RIGHT: Bromeliad blooming in El Yunque National Forest. (Photo by M. Solorzano); Common coquí (*Eleutherodactylus coqui*). (Photo by M. Solorzano); View from El Yunque National Forest looking south to the Caribbean Sea. (Photo by Maria M. Rivera); Mt. Britton trail through Sierra Palm (*Prestoea montana*) stands in El Yunque National Forest. (Photo by Maria M. Rivera); Leaf detail. (Photo by M. Solorzano). BOTTOM: Looking north from Las Cabezas Observation Point in El Yunque National Forest. (Photo by Lisa Jennings).

Product Disclaimer

The use of trade or firm names in this publication is for reader information and does not imply endorsement by the U.S. Department of Agriculture of any product or service.

May 2014
Southern Research Station
200 W.T. Weaver Blvd.
Asheville, NC 28804

www.srs fs.usda.gov

CLIMATE CHANGE EFFECTS
in El Yunque National Forest, Puerto Rico, and the Caribbean Region

Lisa Nicole Jennings, Jamison Douglas, Emrys Treasure, and Grizelle González

View from El Yunque National Forest looking south to the Caribbean Sea. (Photo by Maria M. Rivera)

Preface

Forest lands across the world are experiencing increased risk from extreme weather, drought, fire, insect and plant invasions, and disease. Scientists project increases in air temperature, changes in rainfall patterns, and higher levels of atmospheric carbon dioxide (CO_2) that may cause these threats to occur more often, with more intensity, or for longer durations. Natural resource managers and planners are increasingly tasked with considering the effects of climate change in their everyday work. Although many of the effects of future changes may be considered negative, natural resource management can help mitigate these impacts. Management strategies informed by the best current science enable natural resource professionals to better protect the land and resources and sustain the benefits of forest lands into the future. However, the ever-increasing volume of useful scientific information about climate change makes it difficult for managers and planners to effectively consider and apply emerging science. This report provides a knowledge base of peer-reviewed climate change science for El Yunque National Forest (EYNF), also administratively designated as the Luquillo Experimental Forest (LEF), Puerto Rico, and the greater Caribbean region. The extensive literature review reflects the body of sources gathered by the U.S. Department of Agriculture (USDA) Forest Service's Template for Assessing Climate Change Impacts and Management Options (TACCIMO; Treasure and others 2014) database in collaboration with the International Institute of Tropical Forestry (IITF) and local managers from EYNF.

In the context of increased scrutiny of the effects of climate change on forest resources, the Forest Service, U.S. Department of Agriculture released climate change guidance related to both project-level management operations and large scale forest planning. The recently released *National Forest System Land Management Planning Rule* (USDA Forest Service 2012) requires national forests undergoing land and management plan revisions to complete a broad assessment of available information, including the best available science identified during a thorough review and analysis of relevant peer-reviewed scientific literature. The literature review included in this report aims to address climate change needs for land and resource management planning in EYNF, but it also expands to encompass effects on natural forest lands throughout Puerto Rico and the greater Caribbean region. Content in this report resulted from a comprehensive literature review process, driven by collaboration between TACCIMO's content development staff and technical information specialists and scientists at the IITF library. Direct TACCIMO output, in the form of quotations, was further subject to summarization (see appendix for science summary methodology) and extensive input and review by tropical forest resource specialists from IITF, EYNF, and partner institutions. First, we present an overview of key findings specific to climate change effects on natural resources, focusing on EYNF. Next, we provide a detailed literature review of climate change projections and effects on local drivers and stressors, as well as ecological, physical, social, and economic resources in the Caribbean region. Sources in this report cover over two decades of scientific inquiry, from 1992 to 2013, and reflect the evolving understanding of climate change and its impacts on natural resources, with a focus on new and emerging best available scientific information. In total, we summarized findings from over 240 peer-reviewed literature sources within 16 resource areas. Within each resource area, findings specific to EYNF and Puerto Rico (when available) are indicated by bullet points shaded by a gradient (as in the example below):

• Torres and others (2008) found that the climate of EYNF is sensitive to changes in sea surface temperatures (SSTs). SSTs have increased 1.5 °C over the …

Findings from the broader Caribbean region are indicated by unshaded bullet points.

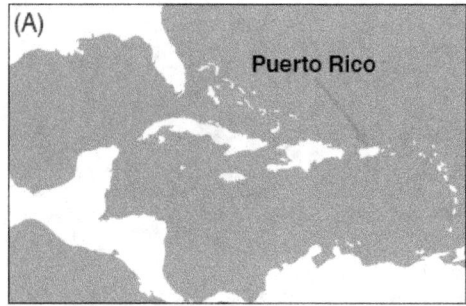

Figure 1—Maps of (A) the greater Caribbean region and (B) Puerto Rico, showing the location of El Yunque National Forest, Pico del Este weather station, and El Verde field station.

Study Region

The greater Caribbean region comprises an area of approximately 2 754 000 km² inclusive of 35 territories and States that border the Gulf of Mexico and the Caribbean Sea. The entire Caribbean region falls within the tropics, geographically delineated by the Tropic of Cancer to the north and the Tropic of Capricorn to the south. Islands are grouped into the Greater Antilles in the north and the Lesser Antilles in the south and east. Puerto Rico, located in the northeastern Caribbean, is the smallest island group in the Greater Antilles with a land area of approximately 9100 km² (fig. 1). Puerto Rico has a tropical maritime climate typical of Caribbean islands (Daly and others 2003). Temperatures are warm year-round, with an island-wide average temperature of 25 °C and seasonal differences of only 3 °C between December and July (fig. 2A; Daly and others 2003). Puerto Rico is influenced by tropical moist systems from June through November and northerly dry systems from December through May, leading to distinct wet and dry seasons (Waide and others 2013). While rainfall averages 1687 mm/year, differences in monthly average precipitation vary between a low of 68 mm in February to a high of 219 mm in October (fig. 2B; Daly and others 2003).

When defined geographically, Puerto Rico's vegetation is considered tropical; however, when defined based on climate variables using Holdridge (1967) life zones, Puerto Rico's vegetation is considered subtropical. Life zone divisions are defined by logarithmic interactions between biotemperature (calculated from average daily temperatures between 0 and 30 °C, using "0" for values below 0 °C and above 30 °C), mean annual precipitation, potential evapotranspiration, and elevation (Lugo and others 1999). In Puerto Rico, life zones include subtropical dry, moist, wet, and rain forests, and lower montane wet and rain forests (fig. 3). Across the island, life zones largely follow precipitation regimes (fig. 2B; Miller and Lugo 2009). Precipitation patterns in Puerto Rico vary widely and are influenced by topography. Mountain ranges create a rain shadow from east to west and north to south as tropical systems move across the island, dropping much of their moisture in the forests

Figure 2—Spatial patterns of average annual temperature (A) and precipitation (B) from 1963 to 1995 based on historic observations. (From Daly and others 2003)

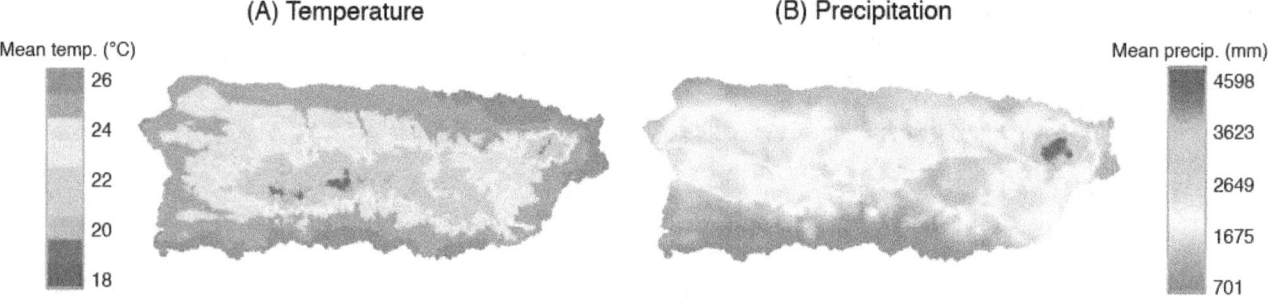

Figure 3—Ecological life zones of Puerto Rico. (From Miller and Lugo 2009)

Subtropical dry forest   Subtropical rain forest

Subtropical moist forest   Lower montane wet forest

Lower montane rain forest   Subtropical wet forest

of the Luquillo Mountains on the northeast end of the island and creating an arid climate in the Guánica dry forest on the southeast end of the island. Elevational gradients also produce large local differences in climate, with lower temperatures and greater precipitation, cloud cover, and humidity with increasing elevation (González and others 2013b). Areas above 600 m in the Luquillo Mountains experience frequent cloud cover and relative humidity near 100 percent due to passing low clouds and the upward transport of moisture from warm Caribbean waters (Weaver 2012). While only six life zones are represented in Puerto Rico, they are characterized by a matrix of many locally recognized vegetation associations (Miller and Lugo 2009).

The 11 310 ha EYNF is located in the Luquillo Mountains of northeast Puerto Rico (fig. 1B) and covers 1.4 percent of the island's area (Weaver 2012). Elevations range from 120 m in the lowlands along the northeast boundary to above 1000 m on mountain peaks. The Luquillo Mountains have a humid tropical maritime climate (Brokaw and others 2012). Due to elevational gradients and geographic position, the climate of the national forest is cooler and wetter than much of Puerto Rico, with temperatures at high-elevation sites averaging 18.5 °C and precipitation averaging greater than 4000 mm annually (Weaver 2012). The forest types of EYNF support a large diversity of tropical species. Dominant life zone distinctions include subtropical wet forests, subtropical rain forests, and subtropical lower montane wet and rain forests (see fig. 3). In EYNF, vegetation types and community structure shift as a result of continuous changes in cloud cover, wind exposure, soil moisture, temperature, and precipitation across an elevational gradient (Brokaw and others 2012, González and others 2013b). Land use histories also vary along the elevational gradient, with land use intensity decreasing with elevation from secondary lowland forests to protected peaks (González and others 2013b). When extreme weather events occur in EYNF, they can have profound effects on vegetation structure and composition (Brokaw and others 2012). Hurricanes frequently pass over the island, generally occurring between July and November, with direct hits to the Luquillo Mountains occurring every 50–60 years (Waide and others 2013). Despite high annual rainfall, severe droughts occur every 15 years on average (Waide and others 2013).

In EYNF, four forest types are locally identified as the dominant vegetation associations, appearing across an elevational gradient (fig. 4; Brokaw and others 2012). Tabonuco (*Dacryodes excelsa*) lower montane wet and rain forests, with tall canopies dominated by tabonuco and motillo (*Sloanea berteriana*), cover undisturbed areas at lower elevations

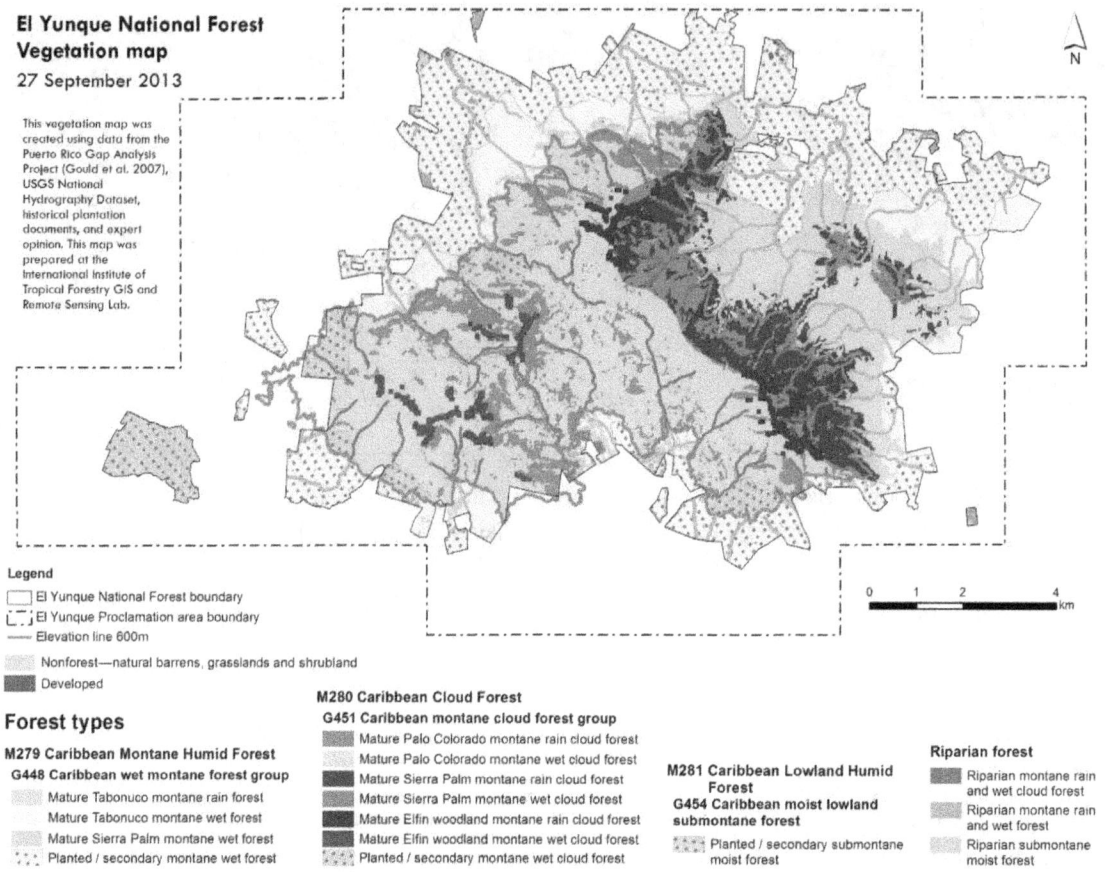

El Yunque National Forest Vegetation map
27 September 2013

This vegetation map was created using data from the Puerto Rico Gap Analysis Project (Gould et al. 2007), USGS National Hydrography Dataset, historical plantation documents, and expert opinion. This map was prepared at the International Institute of Tropical Forestry GIS and Remote Sensing Lab.

Legend
☐ El Yunque National Forest boundary
⌐ ¬ El Yunque Proclamation area boundary
— Elevation line 600m
Nonforest—natural barrens, grasslands and shrubland
■ Developed

Forest types

M279 Caribbean Montane Humid Forest
G448 Caribbean wet montane forest group
Mature Tabonuco montane rain forest
Mature Tabonuco montane wet forest
Mature Sierra Palm montane wet forest
Planted / secondary montane wet forest

M280 Caribbean Cloud Forest
G451 Caribbean montane cloud forest group
Mature Palo Colorado montane rain cloud forest
Mature Palo Colorado montane wet cloud forest
Mature Sierra Palm montane rain cloud forest
Mature Sierra Palm montane wet cloud forest
Mature Elfin woodland montane rain cloud forest
Mature Elfin woodland montane wet cloud forest
Planted / secondary montane wet cloud forest

M281 Caribbean Lowland Humid Forest
G454 Caribbean moist lowland submontane forest
Planted / secondary submontane moist forest

Riparian forest
Riparian montane rain and wet cloud forest
Riparian montane rain and wet forest
Riparian submontane moist forest

0 1 2 4 km

Figure 4—Vegetation communities in El Yunque National Forest. (From Quiñones and others 2013)

between 120 and 600 m. Above the cloud condensation level at 600 m, all vegetation associations are considered cloud forests, characterized by hydric soils, an increased presence of epiphytes, and a higher density of shorter trees and shrubs (Brokaw and others 2012, Weaver 2012). Palo colorado (*Cyrilla racemiflora*) montane wet and rain cloud forests are found in areas between 600 and 900 m, composed mainly of fast-growing and long-lived palo colorado trees. Elfin woodland montane wet and rain cloud forests (also known as dwarf forests) occur on exposed peaks above 900 m, characterized by a single story of stunted, low-canopy trees. Sierra palm (*Prestoea montana*) montane wet and rain cloud forests (also known as palm breaks) are found on steep, east-facing slopes and ravines above 450 m, dominated by disturbance-resistant sierra palms. Beyond the four major vegetation types, planted and secondary submontane and montane forests occur on the edges of the forest boundary, and riparian submontane and montane forests occur along streams and rivers. In addition to diverse ecological communities, the forest supports the headwaters for 10 major rivers that provide drinking water to communities in eastern Puerto Rico, including the nearby San Juan Metropolitan Area (Weaver 2012). Ecological research sites, as part of the Luquillo Experimental Forest designation and the Luquillo Long Term Ecological Research (LTER) program, are established across all forest types, with major studies from the Bisley experimental watersheds and the El Verde field stations in the lower montane forest, and the Pico del Este weather station in the elfin forest.

How to Use this Report

The purpose of this report is to provide a comprehensive and concise summary of the current scientific findings on the effects of climate change on natural resources in Puerto

Rico and the greater Caribbean region to increase understanding and to inform forest planning, as well as to direct subsequent research and climate change vulnerability assessment efforts. Introductory materials provide context in which to consider the findings contained in the report and are not intended to be a comprehensive view of the climatology or ecology of the region. The overview of key findings section provides an executive level summary of climate change effects specific to EYNF and Puerto Rico that is appropriate to use for communication and drawing general conclusions. The body of the report consists of detailed literature review summaries, organized by resource area, which provide more in-depth information across the projected effects of climate change in the Caribbean region. To navigate to a specific issue of interest, the table of contents or keyword searching (Ctrl + F) may be used. The concluding section on knowledge gaps and uncertainties provides a brief examination of overarching research gaps and the likelihood of major climate trends.

Although summarized literature focuses on EYNF and Puerto Rico, the scientific information in this report represents a wide range of ecological communities throughout the greater Caribbean region and the tropics. Comparison among ecological systems necessitates an understanding of underlying environmental conditions at various scales that may be beyond the scope of information presented here (Brokaw and others 2012). Information in this report is summarized from a variety of scientific studies employing varying methodologies and may rely on site-specific measurements, modeling, or professional scientific opinion. Studies presented use varying models and emission scenarios that provide differing and sometimes conflicting projections for the future climatology of the Caribbean, especially in the discussion of precipitation patterns. Some of the predicted effects of climate change lack precision as to when they may occur, and many of the effects may not be seen in local ecosystems until 50–100 years from now. Therefore, it is crucial that the specific information presented in this report is considered within the larger body of climate change science, studies of recent trends, and best practices for natural resource management. In addition, this report does not provide weighting of scientific evidence or discussion of management implications. Literature summaries provided in this report prepare the decisionmaker for further analysis, including engaging the public and local experts through a process that assesses the evidence within the broader context of the management decision, often using best professional judgment and other more qualitative methods (Linkov and others 2009).

Mt. Britton trail through Sierra palm (*Prestoea montana*) stands in El Yunque National Forest. (Photo by Maria M. Rivera)

Contents

Climate Change Effects in El Yunque National Forest, Puerto Rico, and the Caribbean Region

Lisa Nicole Jennings, Jamison Douglas, Emrys Treasure, and Grizelle González

ABSTRACT

Understanding the current and expected future conditions of natural resources under a changing climate is essential to making informed management decisions. However, the ever-increasing volume of useful scientific information about climate change makes it difficult for managers and planners to effectively sort through and apply the emerging science. This report provides a knowledge base of peer-reviewed climate change science for El Yunque National Forest (also administratively designated as the Luquillo Experimental Forest), Puerto Rico, and the greater Caribbean region. We summarized scientific findings from over 240 peer-reviewed sources, covering a wide range of potential effects including changes to drivers and stressors and the effects of climate change on ecological, physical, social, and economic systems. Projected and observed changes include increases in air temperatures, an extension of the dry season, and changes in cloud cover that may lead to significant alterations to the diverse plant and animal communities of the Caribbean region. Species in cloud forests on isolated mountain peaks may be most at risk, due to sensitivities to moisture and a limited chance for migration. Changes in extreme weather patterns, including an increase in hurricane intensity and more frequent drought events, are projected to alter the distribution of tropical forest vegetation. Tourism patterns and recreational opportunities may change with an increase in extreme weather and impacts from sea level rise. The information presented in this report provides a starting point for natural resource managers, planners, and stakeholders to assess the vulnerability of local resources to climate change as part of a broader decision-making framework.

Keywords: Assessment, Caribbean, climate change, El Yunque National Forest, forest planning, Luquillo Experimental Forest, technology transfer.

Overview: Key Findings

Climate Trends

Average temperatures in the Caribbean region have increased over the past 40 years (Uyarra and others 2005). Around the Luquillo Mountains, a small increase in annual maximum and minimum temperatures has been detected in long-term (62-year) records (Waide and others 2013). Scientists predict warming will continue at an accelerated pace (IPCC 2007); however, climate models vary in the degree of warming (table 1). Projected decreases in precipitation in the Caribbean suggest drier wet seasons, and even drier dry seasons (table 2; Cashman and others 2010). Increasing sea surface temperatures may lift the base altitude of cloud formation (Still and others 1999) and alter atmospheric circulation

Looking north from Las Cabezas Observation Point in El Yunque National Forest. (Photo by Lisa Jennings)

Table 1—Climate model projections for increases in temperature at end of century

Source	Spatial extent	Projection
Scatena (1998)	Puerto Rico	+1.5 to +2.5 °C
Girvetz and others (2009), Meehl and others (2007)	Puerto Rico	+2.2 to +2.7 °C
Campbell and others (2011)	Caribbean	+2 to +5 °C
Christensen and others (2007)[a]	Central America	+1.8 to +5 °C
Magrin and others (2007)[b]	Latin America	+1 to +7.5 °C

[a]From the contribution of working group to the Fourth Assessment Report of the ntergovernmental Panel on Climate Change
[b]From the contribution of working group to the Fourth Assessment Report of the ntergovernmental Panel on Climate Change

Table 2—Climate model projections for changes in precipitation at end of century

Source	Spatial extent	Projection
Girvetz and others (2009), Meehl and others (2007)	Puerto Rico	-10 to -30% annually
Campbell and others (2011)	Caribbean	-25% to -50% annually
Biasutti and others (2012)	Caribbean	-30% in spring and summer
Magrin and others (2007)[a]	Latin America	-40% to +10% annually

[a]From the contribution of working group to the Fourth Assessment Report of the Intergovernmental Panel on Climate Change

patterns (Woollings and Blackburn 2012). Any change in the cloud base height will further decrease precipitation in El Yunque National Forest (EYNF) (Comarazamy and González 2011). Climate change may also affect the distribution patterns and concentrations of air pollutants through changing wind and precipitation patterns (Bytnerowicz and others 2007) as well as increased temperatures (Bedsworth 2012).

Extreme Weather

Heavy rainfall events have become more common in Puerto Rico in recent years, particularly since 2009, with changes linked to high sea surface temperatures (Vélez Rodríguez and Votaw 2012). The frequency of extreme precipitation events is expected to continue to increase, leading to potential increases in inland flooding and landslides (Magrin and others 2007, Seneviratne and others 2012). Hurricane events are likely to become less frequent but more severe, with increased wind speeds, rainfall intensity, and storm surge height (Karl and others 2009, Knutson and others 2010). In the Caribbean, the occurrence of very warm days and nights is accelerating, while very cool days and nights are becoming less common (Peterson and others 2002), increasing the likelihood of extreme heat waves (Anderson 2011). Additionally, as annual rainfall decreases over time in the Caribbean region, longer periods of drought are expected in the future (Breshears and others 2005, Larsen 2000). In Puerto Rico, where nearly all wildfires are associated with human activity, the interactions between climate warming and drying and increased human development have the potential to increase the effects of fire (Robbins and others 2008).

Terrestrial Ecosystems

Higher temperatures, changes in precipitation patterns, and any alteration in cloud cover will affect plant communities and ecosystem processes in EYNF (Lasso and Ackerman 2003). Increasing nighttime temperatures may affect tropical tree growth and induce tree mortality (Clark and others 2010, Wagner and others 2012). Both intensified extreme weather events and progressively drier summer months in the Caribbean are expected to alter the distribution of tropical forest life zones (Wunderle and Arendt 2011), potentially allowing low-elevation tabonuco forest species to colonize areas currently occupied by palo colorado forest (Scatena 1998). Because they occur under narrowly defined environmental conditions, EYNF's cloud forests are among the world's most sensitive ecosystems to climate change (Lasso and Ackerman 2003). Cloud forest epiphytes (e.g., bromeliads) may experience moisture stress due to higher temperatures and less cloud cover with a rising cloud base, affecting epiphyte growth and flowering (Nadkarni and Solano 2002, Zotz and Bader 2009). Plant communities on isolated mountain peaks will be most vulnerable, as they will not be able to adapt to the shifting cloud base by moving to higher elevations (Laurance and others 2011, Magrin and others 2007).

Aquatic Ecosystems

Shifts in rainfall patterns due to climate change will lead to periods of flooding and drought that can significantly affect aquatic ecosystems and water resources (Seager and others 2009). Increases in heavy downpours in Puerto Rico and more intense hurricanes in the wet season can lead to greater erosion and sedimentation in waterways (Carpenter and others 1992, Cashman and others 2010, Karl and others 2009). Riparian areas will see changes in structure and composition due to altered temperature, precipitation, and run-off regimes as well as changes in the distribution of plant and animal species (Seavy and others 2009). Extended droughts in the dry season may significantly affect aquatic organisms by decreasing dissolved oxygen (DO) content (Mulholland and others 1997). Freshwater aquatic communities during drought will experience crowding of species, leading to habitat squeezes and a decrease in reproductive output (Covich and others 2003). In EYNF streams, extended periods of extreme low water flows may result in increased pollutant concentrations and excessive nutrients (Cashman and others 2010, Covich and others 2003).

Wildlife

Climatic warming may push the narrow thermal tolerances of many species in tropical environments above their upper limits (Huey and others 2009, Laurance and others 2011), prompting population losses and habitat changes that will affect animal communities (Blaustein and others 2010). Because of their cool-adapted, range-restricted nature, high-elevation amphibians, including Puerto Rican coquí frogs, are especially vulnerable to future changes (Barker and others 2011, Brodie and others 2011, Longo and others 2010, Stallard 2001). More frequent drought conditions may increase the vulnerability of both reptiles and amphibians to water loss, parasites, and diseases including amphibian chytrid fungus (Anchukaitis and Evans 2010, Burrowes and others 2004, Rogowitz 1996). Reduced rainfall may lead to decreased habitat quality for neotropical migratory birds wintering in EYNF (Studs and Marra 2011), while cavity-nesting birds, including the Puerto Rican parrot (*Amazona vittata*), could see an increase in habitat competition and nesting predation with an increase in major hurricane disturbances (Arendt 2000, Pounds and others 1999).

Recreation

The Caribbean region, where year-round warm weather is the principal tourism resource, may see increasing competition from other regions as warm seasons expand globally (Scott and others 2004). Sea level rise will affect coastal resorts, which may affect tourist and recreationist preferences throughout Puerto Rico (Lewsey and others 2004, Magrin and others 2007). Climate change may affect recreation in EYNF through changes to local ecosystems and resources that affect scenic values, as well as changes to weather patterns that may disrupt recreational activities and lead to changes in visitor use (Prideaux and others 2010). Visitors to EYNF may see effects to the local plant and animal communities that make the forest unique (Scatena 1998). An increase in extreme weather events may increase damage to facilities and structures, reduce tourist access in some areas, and increase the need for road repairs (Joyce and others 2008).

Waterfall in El Yunque National Forest. (Photo by F. Scatena)

Sunny day looking west from Mt. Britton tower in El Yunque National Forest. (Photo by Jamison Douglas)

Changes to Drivers and Stressors

Climate Trends

Large-scale circulation patterns

- Torres and others (2008) found that the climate of EYNF is sensitive to changes in sea surface temperatures (SSTs). SSTs have increased 1.5 °C over the last century (PRCCC 2013), and are projected to increase about 1 °C by 2050, with the largest increases in the dry season and the late rainy season (Angeles and others 2007). Increasing SSTs are already causing increased air temperatures in coastal regions of Puerto Rico (Torres and others 2008).
- Temperature patterns in Puerto Rico are influenced by the El Niño/Southern Oscillation (ENSO), while precipitation patterns are largely influenced by the location of the North Atlantic Oscillation (NAO) (Malmgren and others 1998), which occurs in a roughly 60-year cycle (Mazzarella and Scafetta 2012). Climate models project future northward shifts in both mid-latitude and tropical jet streams that will affect the NAO, especially in the winter season (Woollings and Blackburn 2012).[1]

- Future projections using the parallel climate model (PCM) show a decrease in average easterly winds over the Greater Antilles for the coming century, but an increase elsewhere in the Caribbean (Angeles and others 2010).
- A long-term study of climate in the Caribbean (1950–2000) found that trade winds in the early rainfall season have increased in magnitude and shifted to a more easterly or southeasterly flow, with global climate change playing an important role in the trend (Comarazamy and González 2011).
- Observed sensitivities of African dust to changes in climate indicate that future climate change could drastically change the amount of African dust reaching the Caribbean (Prospero and Lamb 2003).

Temperature trends
Historic trends

- At the National Weather Service station in Fajardo, Puerto Rico near the Luquillo Mountains, long-term (62-year) records revealed small but significant increases in annual maximum and annual minimum temperatures (Waide and others 2013).
- In the tropical montane cloud forest at Pico del Este in EYNF, mean monthly minimum temperatures have increased over the past 30 years (Lasso and Ackerman 2003). Similar changes were also found in the Monteverde Cloud Forest Reserve in Costa Rica, where temperatures have increased about 2 °C (LaVal 2004, Pounds and others 1999).
- Using an analysis of weather station data across Puerto Rico from 1900 to present, an average annual increase in temperatures of 0.012 to 0.014 °C per year was observed (PRCCC 2013).
- In the heavily urbanized San Juan Metropolitan Area, air temperatures increased 1.5 °C when compared with similar average past conditions (determined by looking at ENSO indexes) in 1977–1978 (Torres and others 2008).

- Mean annual temperatures in the Caribbean have increased an average of 0.2 to 0.4 °C each decade since 1976 (IPCC 2001, Uyarra and others 2005). Average overnight low and daytime high temperatures have also increased in the Caribbean by 1.0 and 1.8 °C, respectively, since 1950 (Comarazamy and González 2011).

Future trends

- Scatena (1998) modeled a projected increase in temperatures of 1.5 to 2.5 °C in Puerto Rico by the end of the 21st century, while recent studies using regionally downscaled models from Campbell and others (2011) predict a larger increase of 2 to 5 °C in the Caribbean.

---

[1] Within each resource area, findings specific to EYNF and Puerto Rico (when available) are indicated with bulletpoints shaded by a gradient   followed by findings from the broader Caribbean region.

- Using 3rd Coupled Model Intercomparison Project (CMIP3) models from Meehl and others (2007), nonparametric ensembles from Girvetz and others (2009) show average annual increases in temperature of 1.5 °C by 2020, 2.7 °C by 2050, and 4.6 °C by 2090 for Puerto Rico.

- Projections of future climate for the Caribbean region agree that temperatures will increase; yet, the magnitude of increase varies by model and emission scenario as well as regional extent (Biasutti and others 2012, Christensen and others 2007, Magrin and others 2007, Scatena 1998).
- Using the Intergovernmental Panel on Climate Change (IPCC) models, Biasutti and others (2012) projected warmer annual temperatures and lower temperature variability for the future Caribbean climate.
- By 2020, IPCC models project an increase of 0.4 to 1.8 °C in Latin America (Magrin and others 2007).
- The Fourth Assessment Report of the IPCC projects an increase of 1.8 to 5 °C by the end of the century in Central America (Christensen and others 2007). In Latin America, an increase of 1 to 7.5 °C is expected (Galindo and others 2010, Magrin and others 2007).

Precipitation trends
Historic trends

- Across Puerto Rico, rainfall has declined over the 20th century; however, a specific link to climate change has yet to be determined (Waide and others 2013).
- Precipitation in Puerto Rico has varied over the past century, with below-average rainfall measured at 87 percent of the normal for 1990–1997, and 24 percent above the normal in 1998 (Larsen 2000). In Luquillo Experimental Forest (LEF), rainfall decreased an average of 0.20 mm/year from 1988 to 2003 with low rainfall periods most frequently occurring in March (Heartsill-Scalley and others 2007).
- The incidence of heavy precipitation at Pico del Este in EYNF has increased over the past 30 years (Lasso and Ackerman 2003).

- Satellite estimates used by Neelin and others (2006) found a significant drying trend in the Caribbean and Central America since 1950, and point-based estimates show a drying trend of 5–30 percent since 1900. Mid- to long-term data also show drying trends in the Bahamas (10–15 percent since 1959) and Jamaica (11 percent since 1995) (Martin and Weech 2001, Studds and Marra 2011).

Future trends

- Scatena (1998), applying projected future precipitation patterns to the LEF, found that while annual precipitation was projected to remain constant, rainfall variability, including the number of heavy rainfall days, was expected to decrease.
- Nonparametric ensembles from Girvetz and others (2009), using CMIP3 models from Meehl and others (2007), show average annual decreases in precipitation of 5 percent by 2020, 13 percent by 2050, and 16 percent by 2090 for Puerto Rico.

- Recent modeling work for the Caribbean region using the latest IPCC model results suggests a drying trend (Biasutti and others 2012, Campbell and others 2011, Cashman and others 2010).
- Biasutti and others (2012) projected a 30-percent decrease in spring and summer precipitation in the Caribbean using the IPCC ensemble model for the end of the century. Analysis also suggests that the number of consecutive dry days will increase consistent with a lengthening of the dry season, while the number of days with rainfall over 10 mm is expected to decrease (Biasutti and others 2012).

Cloud cover over El Yunque National Forest. (Photo by Lisa Jennings)

- Campbell and others (2011) and Cashman and others (2010), using regionally downscaled climate models, show a decrease in annual rainfall for the Caribbean, with decreases ranging from 25 to 50 percent by the end of the century and the largest decreases in the southern Caribbean (Campbell and others 2011).
- Seasonal projections using regionally downscaled models show drying trends in spring, summer, and fall, with the strongest decreases of up to 35 percent in the summer months (Campbell and others 2011), leading to a drier wet season and even drier dry season, with a potential wet spell in the winter (Cashman and others 2010).
- Future changes in precipitation in the tropics vary by model but also by temporal and spatial extent. Magrin and others (2007) projected a 20-percent reduction to an 8-percent increase in dry season precipitation, and a 30-percent reduction to a 5-percent increase in wet season precipitation for Latin America for 2080. Christenson and others (2007) projected a decrease in precipitation over Central America using the multi-model data set model for the end of the century. Lintner and others (2012) found that the occurrences of both very dry and very wet months are projected to increase in the tropics by the end of the century.
- Using the PCM, Angeles and others (2007) projected a warmer and wetter future climate for the Caribbean region for 2050, with more intense rainfall in the rainy season due to increased SSTs, which increase the amount of available water vapor and a longer and more intense hurricane season (Aguilar and others 2005). However, models for the Caribbean (Neelin and others 2006) and Puerto Rico (Scatena 1998) also predict increasingly severe drought over the next 50 years.

Cloud base trends

- For EYNF, changes to the location of the axis of the convergence zone since 1950 affected orographic lifting mechanisms, which has led to a higher cloud base and strong precipitation reductions during the early rainfall season, ranging from 45 mm at low elevations to up to 150 mm at higher elevations (Comarazamy and González 2011).
- Land cover changes were found to affect the height of the cloud base in the LEF, evidenced by the temporary lifting of the cloud base following the massive defoliation from Hurricane Hugo (Wu and others 2006). However, land use and land cover changes in lowland areas upwind from LEF had little influence on precipitation in the cloud forest, whereas recent conversion from agriculture to forest was found to lower air temperatures (Torres and others 2008).

- A global study of cloud forests using cloud frequency data from 1979–2002 found that the number of cloudy days decreased in cloud forests occurring in the 10°–20° latitudinal band, whereas cloud forests near the equator showed an increase in cloudy days (Bruijnzeel and others 2011).
- Empirical studies indicate that climate change will increase the altitude of the cloud base in tropical mountains due to higher SSTs (Benisten and others 1997, Still and others 1999). This change occurs because warmer seas generate more water vapor and latent heat in the surrounding areas, reducing the changes in temperature with increasing elevation that cause cloud formation (Nadkarni and Solano 2002, Pounds and others 1999). The "lifting cloud base" will decrease inputs of the mist in cloud forests (Nadkarni and Solano 2002) and may alter the forest type's hydrology (Eugster and others 2006).
- In Monteverde Cloud Forest Reserve, Pounds and others (1999) found that dry season mist decreased over the past 30 years, and the mean altitude of the cloud base has risen, owing both to global climate change and widespread lowland deforestation (LaVal 2004). Modeled responses to future climate change project an additional 200-m rise in the cloud base at Monteverde during the dry season (Sill and others 1999).

Extreme Weather

Precipitation extremes

- Heavy rainfall events have become more common in Puerto Rico, particularly since 2009, with changes linked to high SSTs (Vélez Rodríguez and Votaw 2012).
- Historic periods of drought in Puerto Rico, such as the extreme drought experienced from 1993 to 1995, provide a glimpse into future dry periods, which may increase as annual rainfall decreases over time in the Caribbean region (Larsen 2000).
- In northern Puerto Rico, frequently drenched soils and steep slopes contribute to landslide frequency; in the relatively drier south, landslides coincide with intense rainfalls (Lepore and others 2012).

Hurricane Hugo damage at the Bisley experimental watersheds in El Yunque National Forest. (Photo by S. Moya)

- O'Gorman (2012) found a strong correlation between the sensitivity of tropical precipitation extremes to changes in inter-annual temperature variability.
- In the Caribbean, long-term data (since 1950) show that the maximum number of consecutive dry days is falling while measures of extreme precipitation events are increasing (Peterson and others 2002).
- Aguilar and others (2005) found that increases in the percentage of warm days during wet season months (June, July, August, September, October, and November) suggest more insolation and, therefore, fewer cloudy days in Central America and northern South America. Given increased precipitation intensity alone, fewer rainy days and more warm days would be expected (Aguilar and others 2005).
- Though more dry extremes are expected in all seasons of Central America, a limited number of studies have produced estimates of extreme seasonal temperature and precipitation frequencies (Magrin and others 2007).
- Overall, heavy precipitation and dry-spell length in the Caribbean, typified by an intensified hydrological cycle, agree with global averages for extreme temperature and precipitation indices (Aguilar and others 2005, Peterson and others 2002). However, careful interpretation of theoretical arguments for local precipitation time scales is needed; this consideration is important because throughout the tropics, more extreme rainfall and drought counts are mostly affected by wet and dry anomalies, suggesting that there will be increased tropical rainfall spatial gradients (Lintner and others 2012).
- Exacerbating climatic changes, model analyses also indicate a likely increase in drought severity associated with increased deforestation and other land use change (Werth and Avissar 2002).
- Landslides are caused by strong and persistent precipitation events, and in Latin America are linked with deforestation and deficient land planning and disaster contingency schemes (Magrin and others 2007). Thus, many already vulnerable cities will likely experience intensified extreme weather risks and hazards (Magrin and others 2007).

Temperature extremes

- In recent years, an analysis of weather station data (PRCCC 2013) shows that Puerto Rico has experienced an increasing number of hot days > 90 °F, and a decreasing number of days < 75 °F. In 2010 and 2011 alone, 100 days were recorded with temperatures > 90 °F.

- Temperature is expected to increase substantially in tropical forested regions over the next two decades, with seasonal temperature extremes becoming more common (Anderson 2011, Diffenbaugh and Scherer 2011). Unprecedented heat events are expected to occur with increasing regularity at a greater rate in the tropics relative to temperate regions (Anderson 2011).

Hurricane Hugo damage surrounding the Catalina Service Center in El Yunque National Forest. (Photo by S. Moya)

- Projected changes in monthly minimum and maximum temperature extremes are significant in the Caribbean, whereas the rest of the world has shown greater warming in mean monthly minimum temperature. In the Caribbean, the extreme intra-annual temperature range is decreasing, meaning the number of very warm days and nights is accelerating while very cool days and nights are lessening in frequency (Peterson and others 2002).
- Changing temperature extremes from 1960 to 2003 in Central America and northern South America reflect evident warming trends with great spatial coherence (Aguilar and others 2005). Annual percentage of warm days and nights above the 90th percentile maximum have increased 2.5 percent and 1.7 percent each decade, respectively, while the annual percentage of cold days and nights below the 10th percentile minimum decreased at 2.2 percent and 2.4 percent per decade; these warming trends translate to a per-decade rate increase of 0.2 to 0.3 °C in temperature extremes (Aguilar and others 2005).
- Regional cold spells (> 6 days in a row) are lasting 2.2 days per decade less, with most of this trend attributed to pre-1980 climate changes (Aguilar and others 2005).

Tropical storms
Future trends
- O'Brien and others (1992) estimate the expected hurricane frequency in Puerto Rico to be one hurricane every 4 years, causing up to 15-percent tree mortality per storm.

- Numerous climate change studies illustrate the escalating frequency and occurrence of extreme weather events, such as windstorms, tornadoes, hail, heat waves, heavy precipitation, ENSO droughts, or extreme temperature lasting from a few hours to several days (Lewis and others 2009a, Magrin and others 2007).
- Recent studies using IPCC data predict an increase in hurricane intensity in the Atlantic, with higher wind speeds and greater amounts of precipitation, but a reduction in the overall number of storms (Knutson and others 2010, Seneviratne and others 2012). Global projections for the end of the 21st century show a decrease in hurricane frequency ranging from 6 to 34 percent, an increase in wind speed intensity ranging from 2 to 11 percent, and an increase in precipitation intensity ranging from 3 to 30 percent (Knuston and others 2010).
- Global warming may alter the maximum speed of hurricanes, but the ultimate effects on average speed or hurricane frequency are debated, and no evidence shows that hurricane disturbance area will increase (Emmanuel 1987, Lugo 2000).
- Kelman and West (2009) indicate that warmer SSTs and changing storm tracks could cause more tropical storms among Small Island Developing States near the equator.
- Using a simple theoretical model of hurricane intensification under warmer surface water and colder upper tropospheric conditions, Emmanuel (1987) showed that resulting changes in SSTs could increase the damaging potential of hurricanes by a maximum of 60 percent (Hulme and Viner 1998).

Effects of tropical storms on vegetation
- At the El Verde field station, Angulo-Sandoval and others (2004) found that canopy disturbances via hurricanes and droughts increase available light and may—along with associated reductions in herbivorous species—assist in understory shrub and juvenile canopy growth.
- Hurricanes and strong wind storms alter ecosystem structure and organization as well as biogeochemical processes by transferring large quantities of organic matter and nutrients to the soil over short time periods; these changes result in faster short-term decomposition and higher net primary productivity (NPP) (Lugo 2000, O'Brien and others 1992, Silver 1998). Long-term disturbance effects of soil nutrient flux have been observed in the LEF canopy to lead to larger potassium (K) and nitrogen (N) losses (Schaefer and others 2000).

- O'Brien and others (1992), modeling the effects of increased hurricane frequency and intensity over a period of 500 years, found populations of tabonuco and motillo (*Sloanea berteriana*)— two late successional species in LEF— declined at the expense of early successional species. In addition, the risk to vascular epiphytes would be particularly large compared to other tropical vegetation species (Zotz and Bader 2009).
- The high frequency of hurricane disturbances in the Luquillo Mountains causes the accumulating aboveground biomass to be lower than forest stands with smaller frequencies of disturbance. Thus, if disturbances return at intervals shorter than the recovery time of vegetation, less biomass and nutrients will accumulate (Lugo 2000).
- In Puerto Rico's tabonuco forests, hurricane frequency and intensity dramatically affect the density of trees (O'Brien and others 1992) and may influence species diversity, with forests under frequent disturbance attaining lower diversity (based on dominance index values) than those under more periodic disturbance (Doyle 1981). However, topography is an important factor in forests surviving hurricanes, with coves and leeward slopes typically incurring less damage (O'Brien and others 1992).
- Long-term studies following hurricane disturbance in the Bisley experimental watersheds' tabonuco forest found significant changes in both forest structure (Heartsill-Scalley and others 2010) and nonarborescent plant community composition (Royo and others 2011). While plant diversity returned to or exceeded prehurricane levels within 10 years, species composition continued to be altered as vegetation takes time to recover to its original state, particularly when exposed to repeated small-scale disturbance from storms and drought (Heartsill-Scalley and others 2010).
- Royo and others (2011) found a significant increase in fern and vine species in the Bisley experimental watersheds persisting 20 years after Hurricane Hugo.

- Lugo (2000) describes 12 outcomes and effects regarding hurricanes on Caribbean forests: immediate and significant tree mortality, delayed patterns of tree mortality, alternative methods of forest regeneration, successional changes, high species turnover and opportunities for change, diversity of age classes, faster biomass and nutrient turnover, substitution of species, lower aboveground biomass in older vegetation, carbon sinks, selective pressure on organisms, and community structure convergence.
- If hurricane intensity and frequency increase in the Caribbean, landscapes will be set back to earlier successional stages (less mature and more secondary forests), aboveground biomass and height will decrease from interrupted vegetation growth, and disturbance-tolerant species will replace those preferring long, disturbance-free maturing conditions. Decreasing hurricane occurrence and severity would have opposite effects (Lugo 2000).

View to the town of Luquillo, Puerto Rico, from El Yunque National Forest. (Photo by Maria M. Rivera)

Air Quality

Airborne pollutants

- From 1985 to 1998 levels of nitric acid, sulfuric acid, and ammonia deposition increased significantly in the Luquillo Mountains, with the majority of pollutants coming from long-range transport from the northern hemisphere (Stallard 2001). Long-range transport has contributed to the cloud and rainwater chemistry of the Luquillo Mountains (Gioda and others 2013). Subsequent long-term studies (1984–2007) have shown varying trends of pollutant deposition within LEF, with increases in concentrations of pollutants at El Verde field station and decreases at the Bisley experimental watersheds (Gioda and others 2013).
- Mercury deposition at Río Icacos in EYNF is the highest measured in the United States, owing to both dry and cloudwater deposition, but retention of the pollutant is minimal due to high disturbance regimes (Shanley and others 2008).

Fire in a subtropical landscape. (Photo by Dale Wade, Bugwood.org)

- In the Caribbean region, reductions in air quality from long-range transport of dust and other contaminants (Pringle and Scatena 1999)—leading to acid rain and dry deposition (Stallard 2001)—is increasingly becoming an issue.
- Air pollution—particularly from ozone (O_3), nitrogen oxides (N_2O), and mercury (Hg)—is already a major forest stressor in many areas globally. Climate change-induced trends in temperature, precipitation, and atmospheric circulation patterns may increase the severity and duration of air pollution episodes (Bedsworth 2012) and their effects on forests and people (Joyce and others 2008).
- Increases in temperature, in addition to changes in wind patterns and precipitation rates caused by climate change, all have the potential to increase pollutants (Bytnerowicz and others 2007).

Nitrogen deposition

- Nitrogen deposition increased in the Luquillo Experimental Forest at a rate of 0.08 kg nitrogen/ha/year from 1986 to 2004. Assuming current trends continue into the future, Ortíz-Zayas and others (2006) project N_2O emissions to increase in Puerto Rico at an average rate of 7.8 percent per year, with fuel combustion as the primary source of these emissions.
- In a study on the effects of increased nitrogen deposition on soil microbial communities, Cusack and others (2011) found shifts in community structure with increased fertilization, with an increase in fungal abundance at higher elevation sites and an increase in bacterial abundance in lower elevation sites in the Luquillo Mountains.
- Recent studies near San Juan, Puerto Rico have shown that urbanization increases the effects of nitrogen deposition, finding large gradients in soil properties over short distances (Cusack 2013).

- Changes in forest nutrient cycles, especially through increased nitrogen deposition (Mohan and others 2009), may favor certain species and lead to a reevaluation of forest management practices (Bytnerowicz and others 2007).
- Nitrogen deposition is increasing in tropical regions (Cusack 2013), with significant effects on carbon and nutrient cycles in forests (Cusack and others 2011), and is expected to further increase with global climate change (Mohan and others 2009).
- Cusack and others (2012) found that increased fertilization slowed soil respiration rates, increasing the soil carbon pool. However, increased nitrogen deposition also increased the temperature sensitivity of soil respiration, making soil carbon stocks more vulnerable to future warming (Cusack and others 2012).

Fire

- Land use changes will interact with climate change to alter fire regimes in tropical forests (Cochrane and Laurance 2008). In Puerto Rico, where nearly all wildfires are associated with human activity, the feedbacks between climate warming and drying and increased human development have the potential to increase the ecological and economic effects of fire (Robbins and others 2008).
- In Puerto Rico, historical and paleoecological evidence suggests fire frequency is increasing (Burney and others 1994, Robbins and others 2008).
- Studies of fire fuel loading in Puerto Rico and the U.S. Virgin Islands found that the amount of woody debris was lower than other tropical and temperate forests despite the dramatic increase in the amount of fuels and litter following tropical hurricanes (Brandeis and Woodall 2008). Hurricane-induced changes can persist for years and increase future fire risk (Gould and others 2008).

- In moist tropical forests, where fires have been historically rare (Lewis 2006, Silver 1998), an increase in fire frequency from climate change interacting with human-lit fires poses a severe threat to natural ecosystems because very few tree species are adapted to fire (Brodie and others 2011). Thin bark and limited ability to resprout following fire are characteristics of moist tropical forest tree species that make them especially vulnerable to fire (Sherman and others 2008).
- Tropical forest fire frequency has increased over recent decades, with the 1997–1998 ENSO event leading to widespread fires in the tropics (Lewis 2006). If climate change leads to more intense ENSO events as predicted (Yeh and others 2006, 2009), the incidence, magnitude, and duration of fires in the tropics will continue to increase (Brodie and others 2011, Sherman and others 2008).
- Global fire occurrence is projected to rise over the next century with climate change (Flannigan and others 2000), owing to a combination of more frequent cloud-to-ground lightning ignitions and an increase in the conditions that influence the flammability of forest fuels, including temperature, humidity, and precipitation (Brodie and others 2011, Flannigan and others 2000, Sherman and others 2008).
- Fires in cloud forests can be highly destructive, as evidenced by high mortality of canopy trees and extensive consumption of thick organic soils following a fire in a cloud forest in the Dominican Republic (Sherman and others 2008). Severe fires in moist tropical forests have the potential to alter microclimates, allowing noncloud-forest species to invade, which increases the chance of recurrent fires (Sherman and others 2008).

Forest Health

- Climate change will affect disease cycles through changes in host–pathogen interactions in the tropics (Stork and others 2009) and throughout the northern hemisphere and its forests (Joyce and others 2008, Sturrock and others 2011).
- Warmer temperatures are predicted to favor conditions for pathogen development, survival, and disease transmission (Joyce and others 2008), while changes in precipitation will potentially allow pathogens to expand into new areas (Sturrock and others 2011).
- Current global models project a redistribution of insect species under climate change (Logan and others 2003). Warming has been shown to increase insect consumption and movement in a temperate forest (Dukes and others 2008).
- Both insect and disease outbreaks will increase with climate change, as these organisms will be able to accelerate their life cycles and expand their ranges (Joyce and others 2008).

Invasive and Introduced Species

- There are already several invasive species in EYNF, including Africanized bees (*Apis mellifera*) and bamboo (Poaceae family). If Africanized bees increase in the future there will be further competition between the bees and Puerto Rican parrots who utilize the same nesting sites (Blundell and others 2003). Bamboo is already expanding in the forest at a slow pace, and increased flooding in the future could accelerate its spread (Blundell and others 2003).
- Thompson and others (2007) found that populations of introduced species are currently not likely to expand in the LEF; however, this could change with more intense or frequent disturbance. In a study of the introduced species rose apple (*Syzygium jambos*), María (*Calophyllum calaba*), and Arabian coffee (*Coffea arabica*) in LEF, Thompson and others (2007) showed that *S. jambos* is the most likely of the introduced species to increase.
- Increasing intensities of disturbance provide an opportunity for nonnative species planted for farming or ornamental purposes to spread and potentially invade natural forests (Thompson and others 2007). Post-disturbance, the lower mortality rates for introduced species, when compared to native species, allows them to persist (Thompson and others 2007).

Fungi. (Photo by M. Solorzano)

Bamboo, an invasive species in many Caribbean forest areas. (Photo by Forest and Kim Starr, Starr Environmental, Bugwood.org)

- Novel communities of native and introduced species on lands in the Caribbean that have experienced deforestation and then land abandonment can provide clues into how biota may respond in nondisturbed locations to climate change and species invasions (Lugo and others 2012).
- Invasive species movements and expansions may be accelerated by climate change; however, their effects could lead to fewer native species extinctions in tropical forests than in temperate forests (Stork and others 2009).
- Introduced species not historically considered invasive may become invasive under climate change if they experience increased vigor and rate of spread with warmer temperatures and changes in water availability (Hellmann and others 2008).
- In coastal ecosystems in the Caribbean, introduced *Melaleuca* species in swamp forests may be vulnerable to increases in salinity with sea level rise; however, the genetic diversity of the species may allow it to adapt and overcome these increases (Tran and others 2012).

Effects on Ecological and Physical Resources

General Biodiversity

Subtropical and tropical forest ecosystems (general)

- Rising temperatures threaten tropical ectotherms and trees whose thermal-tolerance ranges and acclimation potential are small when compared to their temperate-zone counterparts—i.e., even a lower predicted-temperature increase in the tropics may create a strong biological effect (Brodie and others 2011, Zotz and Bader 2009).
- Pau and others (2011) suggest that species occupying less variable, aseasonal tropical habitats will be forced to shift their ranges or face population declines in future climate regimes. Further, if biotic factors dictate species' phenologies in these areas, there may be high variation in phenology, meaning some species may have a greater ability to adapt to new climate regimes, while other species may be slower in adapting to novel conditions (Pau and others 2011).
- Though climate change adaptation potential may exist within the overall gene pool of a species, the alleles needed for assimilation may be specific to a region or population (Guariguata and others 2008).

The mountains of El Yunque National Forest support a mix of unique plant and animal communities. (Photo by Maria M. Rivera)

Lowland forests

- Conserving lowland forest will minimize the regional effects on climate change associated with deforestation and simultaneously augment the survival of lowland species as they colonize higher elevational gradients (Chen and others 2009).
- In Costa Rican lowlands, increasing temperatures are expected to lead to 30- and 80-percent declines in epiphyte and ant species, respectively (Brodie and others 2011).

Montane cloud forests

- Because of their cool-adapted, range-restricted nature, montane cloud forest endemic species (such as epiphytes and amphibians) are especially vulnerable to increasing insolation and warming, acute heat waves, forest fires, a rising orthogonal cloud base, and less moisture-stripping potential from clouds (Brodie and others 2011, Koopowitz and Hawkins 2012, Lasso and Ackerman 2003, Magrin and others 2007). Thus, these and other tropical montane species are excellent candidates for monitoring the local effects of global climate change (Lasso and Ackerman 2003).
- Changes in temperature are almost certain to have detrimental effects for many tropical montane tree species whose average altitudinal range is 500 m, and animals whose ranges are typically much narrower (Bruijnzeel and others 2011). To keep pace with these changes, montane species are shifting their ranges upslope and may soon be forced beyond their upper elevational limits due to narrow thermal tolerance ranges (Laurance and others 2011).
- Montane forest features that may be affected by rising temperatures include cloud base height, cloud moisture, and pathogen virulence and diversity (Stork and others 2009). Effects include reduced cloud cover, drier conditions, and less water capture potential as climate conditions continue to affect higher elevations (Şekercioğlu and others 2012).
- Because of their smaller geographic spread as well as high energy and area requirements, highland-specialist bird and mammal species are thought to be more prone to extinction than are lower-zone specialist ectotherms and plants (Laurance and others 2011).
- While temperature and humidity changes of cloud forests are expected from climate change, observational and experimental evidence suggests that cloud forest ecosystems may experience additional warming due to deforestation in contiguous lowland areas (Bruijnzeel and others 2011).

Bromeliad blooming in El Yunque National Forest. (Photo by M. Solorzano)

Plant Communities

Subtropical and tropical forest ecosystems (general)

- Wunderle and Arendt (2011) expect that because of global climate change and progressively drier summer months in the Caribbean, new drought-adapted species colonizing the LEF may alter the distribution of life zones and forest types. Additionally, warming trends will likely affect timing of breeding and phenology of flowering and fruiting plants (Wunderle and Arendt 2011).

- Studying plant communities along an elevational gradient in the Sonadora and Mameyes watersheds in the LEF, Barone and others (2008) found that abiotic factors may limit the upper boundary of species, while competition limits the lower boundary. Fog, which has been hypothesized to prompt tropical mountain forest type change, may halt the upward expansion of lowland forest species adapted to more aerobic soil conditions (Barone and others 2008, McGroddy and Silver 2000, Silver and others 1999).

- In unaltered tropical biomes, Brodie and others (2011) suggest that rainforest biodiversity response to rising temperatures has not always been strictly negative. Rapid warming of the Paleocene-Eocene Thermal Maximum event 56.3 million years ago increased floral diversity particularly among epiphytic orchids and ferns. However, it has also been suggested that since tropical plant system response is slow to relatively rapid climate warming, species diversity may decline (Magrin and others 2007), particularly among those plant species with low thermal tolerance occupying high elevational gradients (Laurance and others 2011).

- Increasing atmospheric CO_2 and ambient temperatures are attributed to faster liana (long-stemmed, woody vines) growth and long-term abundance in undisturbed neotropical forests (Guariguata and others 2008).

- As disturbance-adapted liana infestations rise—perhaps due to increasing CO_2 concentrations (Granados and Körner 2002) or elevated stem turnover (Phillips and Gentry 1994)—increased tree mortality, lower stand biomass, and reduced tree growth may be expected (Lewis and others 2004).

- Hannah and others (2011) argue for cautionary interpretation of bioclimatic modeling studies, which suggest high vulnerability of tropical tree species to climate change (Ferreira de Siquiera and Peterson 2003, Hughes and others 1996, Miles and others 2004), because bioclimatic models do not present the full range of conditions under which species can exist. While many tropical species could survive higher temperatures with no current analog, pronounced changes in the moisture balance or higher CO_2 may be harder to withstand (Hannah and others 2011).

Secondary forests

- Land use history influences forest species assemblages in subtropical secondary forests within a set of specific environmental conditions (Brandeis and others 2009). Among the most prominent factors dictating postdisturbance succession of tree and plant communities in Puerto Rico and the U.S. Virgin Islands are spring moisture stress, extreme temperatures, and topographic variables such as elevation and distance from coast (Brandeis and others 2009).

- Due to the exchange in dominance of light-demanding pioneer tree species to shade-tolerant species, Chazdon and others (2005) suggest second-growth forest structure should change faster than mature forests in response to global warming. Therefore, successional dynamics will be helpful in measuring tropical forest response to climate change and land-use and land-cover change (Chazdon and others 2005).

Submontane forests

- Changing climatic conditions themselves are likely to affect lowland species more than are the synergies between climate change and land use (Brodie and others 2011).
- During drought, competition for water and potentially other soil nutrients poses a limiting factor to mature lowland tree growth and survival, increasing susceptibility to mortality (Chazdon and others 2005).
- Tall, range-restricted, tree-form plant species inhabiting closed lowland forests are relatively more threatened by climate change than are the climbing and herbaceous plant species present in multiple tropical regions (Bradshaw and others 2008, Stork and others 2009).
- Tropical lowland nonvascular epiphytes may be severely affected by increasing temperatures because of their precarious carbon balance, which could easily become negative at higher temperatures (Zotz and Bader 2009).
- Tropical lowland lichens and bryophytes may not be able to endure even a minor increase in temperature as these organisms are, arguably, living near to the edge of their physiological capabilities (Zotz and Bader 2009).
- In a cross-species, cross-microhabitat study of moss and liverwort tolerances to altered relative humidity (RH) in French Guiana lowland tropical forest, dry conditions (43 percent RH) resulted in early desiccation of understory bryophytes, whereas the majority of canopy species showed superior desiccation tolerance (Pardow and Lakatos 2013). Thus, canopy species are expected to be able to tolerate drought events and somewhat extended dry seasons of climate change scenarios, while the same conditions are likely to be detrimental to the diversity of understory species (Pardow and Lakatos 2013).

Sierra palm (*Prestoea montana*). (Photo by Maria M. Rivera)

Lower montane forests

- Scatena (1998) interprets the presence of 600-year-old colorado trees (*Cyrilla racemiflora*) occupying isolated proximities well below the cloud base in LEF as evidence of a gradual upward shift in vegetation zonation that has occurred over the past several centuries. The study estimates that whereas a 33-percent increase in annual rainfall would shift the colorado forest species zone down to the boundary of the LEF, either an 11-percent decrease in annual rainfall, a 2.5-°C increase in air temperature, or a 1.1-°C increase in surface temperature would allow the drier, low-elevation tabonuco-type forest species to grow in areas currently occupied by colorado forest types.

- Submontane species expanding their range upslope could place additional resource and habitat pressure on high-elevation species (Brodie and others 2011).
- More seasonal rainfall in lower montane neotropical forests via changing climate regimes would cause a decline in the abundance of the water-impounding Bromeliaceae family (Benzing 1998).

Montane cloud forests

- At the Pico del Este weather station, higher nighttime temperature, increased daytime precipitation, and any alteration in cloud cover can affect plant communities and ecosystem processes (Lasso and Ackerman 2003).

- Because they occur under narrowly defined environmental conditions, tropical montane cloud forests are among the world's most sensitive and vulnerable ecosystems to climate change (Lasso and Ackerman 2003).
- In the absence of changes in vegetation water budget and use, climate change is projected to affect hydrological processes specific to montane cloud forests. Both cloud water index and rainfall interception are likely to be directly affected through changes in fog and rainfall frequency and intensity and indirectly affected through biomass and compositional changes of canopy epiphytes and bryophytes (Bruijnzeel and others 2011).

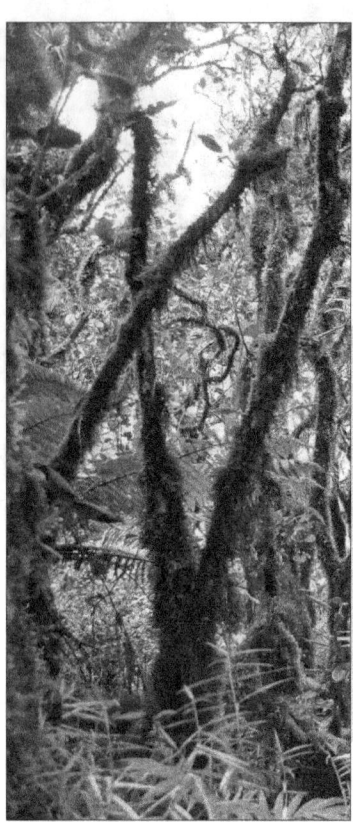

Dwarf (elfin) woodland in El Yunque National Forest. (Photo by Maria M. Rivera)

- A 1- to 2-°C increase in temperature over the next 50 years would raise the altitude of the cloud base during the dry season by 2 m/year and consequently threaten mountainous tropical cloud forest species (Magrin and others 2007). Plants in low, isolated mountains will not be able to adapt to this shifting cloud base temperature gradient and may become locally extinct (Magrin and others 2007).
- Elevated CO_2 levels in nutrient-poor conditions common in cloud forests may decrease photosynthetic capacity and may alter flowering plant phenology and gene expression (Lasso and Ackerman 2003).

Cloud forest epiphytes

- Though the most important environmental constraint for vascular epiphytes is water availability, Olaya-Arenas and others (2011) found the flowering of the orchid *Lepanthes rupestris* in the LEF to be temperature dependent. Given projected warming, they expect a dramatic reduction in the quantity of reproductive individuals and population growth rates of *L. rupestris*, which will in turn affect seeding production, future recruitment, and reproductive capacity.
- At Pico del Este, over the last 30 years Lasso and Ackerman (2003) found an increasing mean minimum temperature to be correlated with bromeliad (*Werauhia sintenisii*) induction and a later flowering season.
- Lasso and Ackerman (2012) found that increasing temperatures that boost nutrient deposition from forest litter fall may raise the reproductive output of one major component in a vascular epiphyte community in Pico del Este. Thus, higher temperatures resulting in faster organic soil decomposition may promote epiphyte growth and reproduction unless water becomes the primary limiting factor.

- In cloud forest ecosystems, epiphyte loss due to climate change is almost certain, as epiphytes are restricted to the atmospheric-terrestrial interface (Nadkarni and Solano 2002) and thus are highly sensitive to changes in growing conditions (Benzing 1998).
- Climate change will threaten cloud forest epiphytes through increased dryness, due to both higher temperatures and less moisture through cloud water, as the cloud base altitude rises (Pounds and others 1999, Still and others 1999, Zotz and Bader 2009). Experimental evidence suggests reduced cloud cover can also directly affect epiphyte longevity and productivity (Nadkarni and Solano 2002).
- Altitudinal increases in the height of cloud banks and increased evapotranspiration will affect epiphytes most in the dry season, when cloud forests rely heavily on the deposition of cloud droplets (Zotz and Bader 2009).
- Uncharacteristically warm nights or the lack of adequate cooling after sundown may subject plants that fix carbon through Crassulacean Acid Metabolism photosynthesis (e.g., epiphytic bromeliads) to net carbon losses under otherwise adequate growth conditions (Benzing 1998).
- In an 18-month experiment at Monteverde Cloud Forest Reserve, epiphyte exposure to environments with gradually less cloud water—a scenario synonymous with expected ecosystem changes in global climate models—led to a generally negative effect on epiphytic taxa growth, with severity depending on the season of transplant and plant species (Nadkarni and Solano 2002). It is predicted that climate change will not only decrease epiphyte growth and leaf production and increase mortality, but will alter the composition of canopy communities by releasing terrestrial plant seed banks within arboreal soils; this could create conditions suitable for only the most desiccation-resistant epiphytes (which now occupy low elevation forests) in the canopy of upper cloud forests (Nadkarni and Solano 2002).

Animal Communities

General effects

- Martín González and others (2009) found that rainfall and temperature are significant determinants of pollinator composition and importance in the West Indies islands of Puerto Rico, Dominica, and Grenada, with rainfall being the key driver of pollinator variation. Comprehending how these determinants and other dynamics of future climate change influence pollinator processes is vital (Martín González and others 2009).

- According to Stork and others (2009), species traits that indicate risk from climate change include: low population densities, narrow niches, low vagility, small range, mature-habitat specificity, large body size, and those dependent on other species for food. Large vertebrates are especially vulnerable.
- Tropical species often have narrow thermal tolerances and may be already living close to their upper thermal limits (Gunderson and Leal 2012, Huey and others 2009, Laurance and others 2011).
- Deutsch and others (2008) investigated four groups of tropical terrestrial vertebrate ectotherms (insects, frogs, lizards, and turtles) and found that tropical species will reach their critical maximum temperature proportionally faster than similar high-latitude species, despite the tropic's lower absolute rates of warming (Deutsch and others 2008). Deleterious thermal performance changes are likely in tropical members of all four taxonomic groups (Deutsch and others 2008, Dillon and others 2010, Tewksbury and others 2008).
- Pounds and others (1999) found in the Monteverde Cloud Forest Reserve that the interplay of changes in water availability and varying large-scale climate processes, such as the ENSO, may induce population losses among amphibians and reptiles as well as habitat and biological changes in the bird community, as drier warming periods are correlated with such observed changes (Blaustein and others 2010).

Common coquí (*Eleutherodactylus coqui*). (Photo by M. Solorzano)

Amphibians

- Predictions of changing environments and increased hurricane intensity and drought frequency make high-elevation (> 1000 m) Puerto Rican coquí frogs, upland coquí (*Eleutherodactylus portoricensis*) within the Luquillo and Cayey Mountains (Barker and others 2011), and common coquí (*Eleutherodactylus coqui*) within the Luquillo Mountains (Longo and others 2010, Stallard 2001) particularly vulnerable to future climate change.
- Stewart (1995) showed that rather than total monthly or annual rainfall, it is the distribution of rainfall or the prolonged periods of drought that significantly impact *E. coqui* population densities in the LEF, especially among juveniles.
- Between 1979 and 1989, *E. coqui* declined at the El Verde field station (Stallard 2001). In the past three decades, three species of endemic anurans (frogs and toads) have become extinct (Longo and others 2010), while long-term amphibian monitoring data revealed eight populations of six different species declined in EYNF between 1990 and 2000 (Longo and others 2010).
- Ospina and others (2013) studied calling patterns of four *Eleutherodactylus* species in a wetland near Toa Baja, Puerto Rico and found variations in species response to weather variables. Calling activity of *E. coqui* and *E. cochranae* (whistling coquí) was positively correlated with temperature, while calling activity of *E. brittoni* (grass couqí) and the endangered *E. juanariveroi* (plains coquí) was negatively correlated with temperature and precipitation. Future climate change could threaten all four of these species, with more intense pressures on the sensitive *E. brittoni* and *E. juanariveroi* (Ospina and others 2013).

Puerto Rican parrot (*Amazona vittata*). (Photo by USDA Forest Service).

- From 1970 to 2000, Burrowes and others (2004) found a significant increase in temperature each month from May to October, the warm/wet season peaks of amphibian activity in Puerto Rico. Along with increased temperature and dry season length, Donnelly and Crump (1998) suggest decreased soil moisture and increased inter-annual rainfall variability will strongly affect neotropical amphibians at individual, population, and community levels. They found that if a hotter, drier, less predictable climate decreases leaf-litter anurans' main food supply (invertebrates), juveniles will have stunted growth rates and adults may devote less energy to reproduction (Donnelly and Crump 1998).

- Anuran declines and extinction may be associated with synergistic patterns of climate change and chytrid fungus (*Batrachochytrium dendrobatidis*) (Anchukaitis and Evans 2010, Hannah and Lovejoy 2011) and the extension of the dry season (Barker and others 2011, Burrowes and others 2004), as well as increasing temperatures at higher elevations (Brodie and others 2011) and low precipitation in cloud forests (Magrin and others 2007). It is likely these anurans and other restricted-range amphibian species of tropical Central America will experience high turnover rates as conditions simultaneously become hotter and drier (Blaustein and others 2001).

- Suboptimal temperature and humidity regimes induced by climate change negatively affect amphibians' behavior and energy budget and alter host–parasite relationships (Donnelly and Crump 1998, Pounds and others 1999). Shifting conditions in montane areas of Central and South America create nighttime temperatures closer to the thermal optimum for chytrid fungus proliferation, while increased daytime cloud cover prevents frogs from finding pathogen refuges (Blaustein and others 2010).

- Loss of suitable habitat and drought conditions (Longo and others 2010) cause anurans to clump around remaining moist areas, making them more vulnerable to disease (Burrowes and others 2004) and, in particular, the chytrid fungus (Anchukaitis and Evans 2010).

- Pond-breeding neotropical anurans will likely experience compression of the breeding season and more competition for moist sites suitable for oviposition, leading to more species using a pond simultaneously and higher mortality in early life stages (Donnelly and Crump 1998). Sporadic breeders will be least affected by climate changes altering pond hydrology while prolonged breeders, where male reproductive success is tied to tenure at the breeding site, will be most affected. Explosive breeders, being better adapted to reproduce under high density conditions in a short period of time, will likely be less affected than prolonged breeders. In general, narrowly endemic amphibians will see additional pressures with pond drying (Donnelly and Crump 1998).

- While drier conditions might reduce the likelihood of fungal attack on arboreal amphibian eggs, this could be offset by an increase in parasitic drosophilid fly (family Drosophilidae) attacks (Donnelly and Crump 1998).

- Amphibians may become more susceptible to or be killed by warming-induced acid rain, fog, and other types of airborne and stream contamination (Carey and others 2001, Stallard 2001).

Birds

Habitat alterations

- Smith and others (2010) utilized a satellite-derived index of habitat moisture at the Roosevelt Roads Naval Station on the east coast of Puerto Rico to assess the underlying gradient of northern waterthrush (*Seiurus noveboracensis*) habitat quality. They found that extreme-wet-habitat specialists, such as *S. noveboracensis*, are quite vulnerable to even slight deviations of annual precipitation, especially during El Niño and La Niña cycles (Smith and others 2010).

- Endothermic tropical birds are more likely to be indirectly affected by climate change via its effects on community vegetation and food sources, rather than via direct physiological effects (Şekercioğlu and others 2012).

- Though it is possible for tropical bird species living in coastal or island habitats to cope with a 2-°C increase in average temperature, more extreme tropical weather events could destroy critical habitat or make foraging impossible (Şekercioğlu and others 2012).
- As habitat availability, food, and shelter resources become constrained by warming, tropical highland birds' elevational ranges narrow and extinction risk increases (Şekercioğlu and others 2012). Climate warming in the montane cloud forests of Costa Rica has raised the average altitude at the base of the orographic cloud bank (Pounds and others 1999), resulting in the colonization of the tropical cloud forest by bird species from lower altitudes (Crick 2004).
- Winter habitat quality for neotropical migratory birds is expected to be reduced by the projected drying of the Caribbean islands (Rodenhouse and others 2008, Studds and Marra 2011).
- Sea level rise, worsened by tropical storms, may convert some dynamic wetland areas into salt pans, lessening the likelihood of tropical bird colonization (Şekercioğlu and others 2012).
- Climate change-induced alterations in soil properties of moist tropical forests will decrease net available moisture, changing the forest biochemistry into tropical savannah rather than dry forests (Toms and others 2012). For birds in tropical dry forests, climate change can increase the rate of habitat loss by introducing stressors such as fire, invasive species, parasites, or disease (Toms and others 2012).

Population and survival

- In the short term, hurricane-induced mortality may constrain tropical bird populations of the LEF below the recovery threshold, particularly the endangered Puerto Rican parrot because of its confined range, small population size, and low growth rate (Wunderle and Arendt 2011). However, in the long term, hurricanes may be beneficial to bird populations with adequate size because of increased nutrient cycling and nest cavity creation (Wunderle and Arendt 2011).
- The abundance of migratory ovenbirds (*Seiurus aurocapilla*) in the Guánica dry forest in southwest Puerto Rico decreased in response to increased summer rainfall in the United States. Similarly, wintering black-and-white warblers (*Mniotilta varia*) and American redstarts (*Setophaga ruticilla*) saw decreases in survival with increasing amounts of the previous year's first six months of rainfall in the United States. (Dugger and others 2004).
- Faaborg and others (2013) also found significant declines in the wintering populations of *S. aurocapilla*, *M. varia*, and *S. ruticilla*, as well as declines in the overall diversity of neotropical migrant birds in Guánica Forest. Winter survival rates remained steady over time, meaning that declining populations are due to a decline in recruitment of birds at the site, possibly due to habitat quality changes induced by climate change that has led birds to winter elsewhere (Faaborg and others 2013).

- Though they enjoy longer lifespans than temperate birds, tropical birds are comparatively more vulnerable to climate change because of their smaller clutch size, less active nature, and lower tolerance of climatic variability (Şekercioğlu and others 2012). Moreover, tropical bird specialists are considered to be more vulnerable to climate change than are generalists (Toms and others 2012).
- Şekercioğlu and others (2008) provides that sedentary tropical birds are five times more likely to face climate change-induced extirpation in the 21st century than are long-distance migrants.
- Nearly 80 percent of bird species restricted to tropical dry forests are considered to be at risk for climate change alterations (Toms and others 2012).

Behavioral responses

- As shown by Arendt (2000, 2006), following major hurricane alteration of forest vegetation, nest predation by rats, nest usurpation by swarming bees, and the prevalence and intensity of philornid ectoparasites increased in nests of *A. vittata* (Puerto Rican parrots) and a surrogate study species, the pearly-eyed thrasher (*Margarops fuscatus*). Thrasher reproduction, survival rates, and predator response differed between Hurricanes Hugo (1989) and Georges (1998) (Wunderle and Arendt 2011).
- Merola-Zwartjes and Ligon (2000) found that Puerto Rican todies (*Todus mexicanus*) from the Guánica dry forest had significantly lower basal metabolic rates than did those from the cooler rain forest site at LEF. While a lower rate of endogenous heat production is typical in species inhabiting warm environments compared to the same species in cooler climates (Dawson and O'Connor 1996), Guánica *T. mexicanus* should benefit from lower basal metabolic rates because of reductions in both the potential for heat loading and the need for evaporative cooling (Merola-Zwartjes and Ligon 2000).

- Cavity-nesters (owls, woodpeckers, and parrots) should expect more competition for remaining tree hollows from both tropical birds and cavity-dwelling mammals. According to Pounds and others (1999), in Monteverde Cloud Forest Reserve, keel-billed toucans (*Ramphastos sulfuratus*) are nest predators that have recently expanded their range into montane highlands, where they both compete for sites with resplendent quetzals (*Pharomachrus mocinno*) and prey on their nests.
- Many tropical birds, such as the white-throated thrush (*Turdus assimilis*), prefer to breed in the wet season due to the abundance of resources. Since climate change causes increasingly longer and variable dry seasons and droughts, migratory and reproductive routines of tropical birds may be affected, and populations may decline (Şekercioğlu and others 2012).
- Pounds and others (1999) observed that from 1973 to 1998 the distribution of lower and pre-montane bird species in Monteverde Cloud Forest Reserve, Costa Rica shifted upslope and back downslope an average rate of 19 species per decade, with present lower-montane species remaining stable and pre-montane species increasing.
- Isotope research by Fraser and others (2008) in Nicaragua showed that several partial-frugivore species, including pollinators such as hummingbirds, make yearly altitudinal migrations, which may be greatly impacted by global warming.
- Studds and Marra (2011) found in southwest Jamaica that *S. ruticilla* (American redstarts) adapted the timing of their spring migratory patterns in relation to an increasingly severe and unpredictable winter dry season. Birds migrating between North America and the Caribbean must therefore attempt to breed earlier, contending with fewer and more variable winter food resources (Studds and Marra 2011).
- In the West Indies islands of Dominica, Grenada, and Puerto Rico, Martín González and others (2009) found that although there was no significant relationship between tropical bird pollinator richness and importance and climatic factors, birds visited a higher proportion of plant species and played a more central role in the pollinator network towards the wet end of the rainfall gradient. Thus, for the Caribbean as in Central and South America, birds tend to become more important as pollinators as rainfall increases (Martín González and others 2009).

Reptiles

- Traits such as core temperature and maximum critical thermal temperature of some Puerto Rican *Anolis* species vary over altitudinal gradients, while other species, such as the Puerto Rican yellow-chinned anole (*Anolis gundlachi*), from El Verde field station and El Yunque peak sites, show no trait variation (Rogowitz 1996). The ability of *Anolis* to thermally adapt their metabolism to changing ambient temperatures may be weak to negligible (Gunderson and others 2011). In 14-day experiments at El Verde and El Yunque sites, *A. gundlachi* experienced no change in metabolism from exposure at 15 °C lower than usual, but suffered a significant decline in metabolism and a consequent loss of body mass from exposure to temperatures 30 °C above normal (Rogowitz 1996).

- Huey and others (2009) utilized observational data and a conservative 100-year increase of 3 °C over 1970 temperatures to assess body temperature responses of lowland *Anolis* and S*phaerodactylus* lizards living in Puerto Rican forests, many of which are already experiencing temperatures beyond their thermal safety margins. They found many tropical lowland lizards are at risk from even a small increase in operative temperatures because convection dominates heat exchange in forests (body temperatures increase at the same rate as air temperatures) and the thermal environment is already warm relative to lizard's thermal sensitivity (Gunderson and Leal 2012, Huey and others 2009).
- While increased summer heat stress is likely to reduce daily activity time and sprint performance of Puerto Rican lizards, particularly during midday, warmer winters will create more favorable reproductive conditions (Huey and others 2009). Moreover, some species residing in high-latitude or cool montane forest environments should benefit with increased activity times and growth rates (Huey and others 2009). Gunderson and Leal (2012) show that in assuming a 3-°C increase in ambient temperature, the mean performance capacities of the Puerto Rican crested anole (*Anolis cristatellus*) in dry, sparsely vegetated xeric habitats of Puerto Rico are predicted to decrease by 26 to 32 percent, while mean performance of lizards in cool, vegetated mesic habitats should expect an increase of 3–5 percent.
- Gunderson and others (2011) suggest that acclimation alone does not sufficiently account for patterns of water loss rate variation found between populations of the *A. cristatellus* in Cambalache and Guánica dry forests. Supporting literature of the few lizard species studied thus far show negative correlations between arid habitats and water loss rates even if lizards from each species population are exposed to identical climatic conditions preceding water loss measurement (Gunderson and others 2011, Hertz and others 1979, Hillman and others 1979, Perry and others 2000).

Crested anole (*Anolis cristatellus*). (Photo by Kevin Enge, Florida Fish and Wildlife Conservation Commission, Bugwood.org)

- Climate warming may cause tropical forest lizards to suffer increased predation and competition from warm-adapted, open-habitat lizards such as the mid-American ameiva (*Ameiva festiva*) (Huey and others 2009).
- Two highland anoline lizard populations (the cloud forest anole and montane anole) in Monteverde Cloud Forest Reserve declined since the increase in the number of mist-free days in the late 1980s and disappeared by 1996, whereas the gray lichen anole (*Anolis intermedius*) remained stable being better adapted to warmer, drier conditions (Pounds and others 1999).
- Smaller body size makes individual lizards more prone to water loss, thus affecting their ecology, especially in water-restricted tropical locations such as Guana Island of the British Virgin Islands (Nicholson and others 2005).
- In a study by Patiño-Martínez and others (2012), sex ratios in hatchlings of leatherback sea turtles (*Dermochelys coriacea*) in the southwestern Caribbean Sea were clearly female skewed by an average of 92 percent over three nesting periods. Backed by previous research that establishes patterns of thermal sensitivity for gender determination (Godley and others 2001, Hawkes and others 2009), their model predicts that increased temperatures via climate warming could lead to a complete feminization of hatchlings within a decade. However, deeper and smaller nesting sites lower on the shore on lighter colored beaches, where metabolic heating effects would be less detrimental, could create conditions more appropriate for future male hatchling sea turtle succession (Patiño-Martínez and others 2012).

Invertebrates

- Microclimate and soil characteristics are more likely to be significant determinants of terrestrial gastropod distributions than are the indirect influences of vegetation, which provide gastropods with habitat structure and resources (Presley and others 2011). In

La Coca Falls in El Yunque National Forest. (Photo by Lisa Jennings)

the LEF, Hurricanes Hugo (1989, category 3) and Georges (1998, category 3) caused a relocation of biomass from canopy to the forest floor, which increased the resource base for terrestrial gastropods but unfavorably altered microclimate conditions (Bloch and Willig 2006).

- As observed in mosquito larval habitats of Río Piedras, Puerto Rico, sequences of rainfall followed by lack of rainfall have led to sharp population declines of mosquitoes (*Aedes aegypti*) (Chaves and others 2012). Even though the study demonstrates that population outbreaks are largely correlated with extreme climatic events, Chaves and others (2012) contend that the observed mosquito population dynamics support neither the linear predictions of increased mosquito abundance, nor the claim that dynamics can be swayed by vector control programs.

- In the West Indies islands of Puerto Rico, Dominica, and Grenada, richness, plant interaction, and importance of bee species within the pollinator community decreased with increased rainfall, while dipterans' (true flies) importance increased with rainfall, thus partially replacing one another as major insect pollinators (Martín González and others 2009). Meanwhile, wasps benefited from increased species richness with higher rainfall, and lepidopterans (butterflies and moths) showed no significant trend with rainfall or temperature (Martín González and others 2009).
- In species- and assemblage-level analyses, Chen and others (2009) showed a steady increase in the average elevation of moths on Mount Kinabalu, Borneo between 1965 and 2007, with the average elevation of species rising 67 m. The findings of an uphill shift in habitat, coupled with previous research of tropical insect thermal sensitivity (Addo-Bediako and others 2000, Deutsch and others 2008, Jazen 1967), indicate that tropical insects, given their diversity, may dominate species threatened with extinction from climate change (Chen and others 2009).

Mammals

- Increased tropical extreme weather event frequency has a marked, yet species-specific, deleterious effect on bat populations, principally among tree-roosting bats; this effect is attributed to tree loss and more native hunting rather than direct hurricane mortality (Jones and others 2009). Research (Gannon and Willig 2009) suggests the recovery rate of the Puerto Rican cave-roosting Jamaican fruit bat (*Artibeus jamaicensis*) depends on hurricane severity, with recovery occurring more rapidly after Hurricane Hugo (1989, category 3) than after Hurricane Georges (1998, category 3), while populations of tree-roosting, red fig-eating bats (*Stenoderma rufum*) declined after Hugo.

- Increased temperatures may also impact bat populations. In Costa Rica, LaVal (2004) found no net change in the number of bats captured in Monteverde Cloud Forest Reserve over a 27-year period, but revealed a growing number of lowland bat species at higher elevations—a phenomenon hypothesized to be due to the climatic effects resulting from a 2-°C increase in minimum temperatures (Pounds and others 1999).

Freshwater (Aquatic and Riparian) Ecosystems

- For two species of freshwater shrimp (*Atya lanipes* and *Xiphocaris elongate*) in the LEF, Covich and others (2003) observed a two- to three-fold increase in average shrimp densities within upper-altitude pools due to the effects of droughts. This has led to severe crowding and hence less reproductive success for shrimps as well as a significant shift in the size-class distribution.
- When the migratory "cue" of flowing water is barred from juvenile freshwater shrimps, they are impounded in low-elevation bottlenecks, making them prey for fish and birds (Crook and others 2009). During the drought year of 1994 in EYNF, poor streamflow and low stream connectivity limited the ability of shrimp larvae and juveniles to advance to

the next life stage (Crook and others 2009). In the same drought year, the lowest mean abundance of palaemonid river shrimp (*Macrobrachium* spp.) in 28 years was recorded in the Espiritu Santo drainage of the Luquillo Mountains, with hurricane and storm flows having relatively little effect on population (Covich and others 2006).

- Due to climate change, extended droughts in tropical rainforests may significantly affect freshwater aquatic communities through crowding of species, leading to habitat contraction and a decrease in reproductive output (Covich and others 2003).
- Warmer temperatures, in combination with altered flows due to increased drought, may limit dissolved oxygen (DO) availability in freshwater environments by promoting macrophyte growth including algal blooms (Cashman and others 2010, Ficke and others 2007). High macrophyte growth rates may also lead to sediment trapping and excess nutrients (Ficke and others 2007).
- Extended droughts in the dry season may significantly affect aquatic organisms by decreasing DO content (Mulholland and others 1997).
- Riparian areas will see changes in structure and composition due to altered precipitation and run-off regimes, as well as changes in the distribution of plant and animal species (Seavy and others 2009).
- Globally, riparian areas will play an important role under climate change by providing thermal refugia for sensitive species; this is based on the riparian area's ability to buffer against extreme temperatures due to high water content and shade provided by dense vegetation (Seavy and others 2009).

Icacos River in El Yunque National Forest. (Photo by F. Scatena)

Water Resources

Water balance
- Scatena (1998) found that projected future changes of increased temperatures and precipitation could change vegetation types in LEF and alter forest-wide hydrology. If the tabonuco-type forest expands upslope into the area currently inhabited by the palo colorado-type forest, forest-wide runoff could decrease as much as 17 percent due to the lower runoff rates for the tabonuco-type (Scatena 1998).
- Harmsen and others (2009) modeled the effects of climate change on groundwater in Puerto Rico and found that projected large increases in precipitation for the rainy season will produce a net increase in annual aquifer recharge, whereas projected decreases in precipitation in the dry season will have minimal effect. An increase in aquifer recharge suggests that groundwater levels could increase, reducing saltwater intrusion in some coastal aquifers (Harmsen and others 2009).

- The effect of climate change on the water balance in cloud forests is largely influenced by changes in rainfall (Bruijnzeel and others 2011).
- Changes in evapotranspiration due to increased temperatures could decrease runoff, even in dry regions (Galindo and others 2010).

Water quantity and quality
- Climate change is likely to amplify existing pressures on water resources and water availability in northeastern Puerto Rico, especially in combination with increased urban development and water extraction (Crook and others 2007).
- More intense rainfall events lead to increased runoff in the wet season; these events can also lead to decreased water quality through increased turbity and erosion as well as flooding (Cashman and others 2010). Watersheds that respond quickly to precipitation, such as in the Luquillo Mountains, may be especially affected (Schellekens and others 2004).
- As a small island, freshwater resources in Puerto Rico will be affected not only by changes in precipitation, but also by changing hurricane cycles and saltwater intrusion from sea level rise (Kelman and West 2009).

Soil showing anaerobic conditions and biological activity in the cloud forest of El Yunque National Forest. (Photo by Maria M. Rivera)

- Although overall precipitation levels in the Caribbean may remain similar in the future, dry years and water shortages may become more frequent or more severe (Biasutti and others 2012) as the rainy season becomes wetter and the dry season becomes drier (Harmsen and others 2009).
- Extended periods of extreme low flows in the dry season may result in increased pollutant concentrations and excessive nutrients in Caribbean streams (Cashman and others 2010, Covich and others 2003).

Soil and Geologic Resources

Soil health

- Soils in the Luquillo Mountains will be affected by climate change through increased variability in the decay of organic matter, changes to the patterns of soil oxygen concentrations, and changes in the accessibility of soil nutrients to plants (González and others 2013a).
- The Luquillo Mountains receive deposits of African dust that can change the composition and texture of soils, potentially affecting nutrient storage. Projected increases in African dust deposits with climate change may further affect soils on mountain peaks (González and others 2013a, Ping and others 2013).
- In the LEF, soil oxygen content decreased significantly with increasing annual rainfall, exhibiting soil oxygen levels below half of ambient concentrations in > 30 percent of palo colorado-type forests and > 60 percent of elfin cloud forests studied over the 18-month period (Silver and others 1999). Soil oxygen concentration was consistently found to be responsive to both long-term annual and short-term precipitation events (Silver and others 1999).
- Silver (1998) found that riparian microsite soil conditions in the LEF shifted between predominately aerobic and anaerobic in relation to 14-day rainfall cycles; aerobic soils supported relatively more plant biomass but less soil organic carbon (SOC) and nutrient availability, whereas anaerobic soils became a net source of CH_4 (methane).
- Puerto Rican soils in the oxisols and ultisols classes may experience losses in soil organic matter due to temperature- and/or rainfall-induced water stress, implying that a lengthening dry season is likely to impact tropical forest soils, the resident vegetation, and the associations and interactions between them (Silver 1998).

- In tropical forests, seasonal soil decomposition is closely tied to wetting and drying cycles, suggesting that seasonal adjustments in temperature and moisture due to climate change are likely to affect decomposer communities, soil resource quantity and distribution, and litter quality (Silver 1998).
- The negative correlation found by Silver (1998) between litter fall and elevation is likely an indirect response to a changing climate, as less litter fall is associated with a lower temperature. Since litter fall and decay rates are tightly coupled with nitrogen (N) and phosphorus (P) cycles, tropical ecosystem decay may be vulnerable to temperature changes (Silver 1998).
- Under conditions of higher temperature and CO_2 supplement, soil respiration and net primary productivity (NPP) will be affected by water and nutrient availability (Silver 1998). An expected increase in CO_2 levels is likely to have a significant impact on the biogeochemical cycles of tropical ecosystems (Silver 1998).
- Prolonged drought could disrupt and decouple the highly synchronized nutrient cycles of tropical wet forest ecosystems and exacerbate nutrient stress in water-inhibited areas. On the other hand, greater precipitation quantity and frequency in dry tropical forests will likely increase decomposition rates as well as nutrient availability and uptake (Silver 1998).

Soil carbon and trace gas dynamics

- Under the climate change scenario of increasing temperature and decreasing rainfall (Scatena and Lugo 1998), simulation results from Wang and others (2002) provide that higher and lower elevations of the LEF can expect losses in soil organic carbon (up to 4.5 Mg/ha), while middle elevations will experience smaller increases (up to 2.3 Mg/ha). These findings suggest the effects of climate change on soil decomposition and SOC storage and flux will not be uniform across elevations (Wang and others 2002) because of the indirect effects of temperature and precipitation (McGroddy and Silver 2000).

- Over the entire LEF, Wang and others (2002) found significant differences in simulated total SOC storage from low elevations of tabonuco-type forests (20 Mg/ha) to high elevations of the elfin-type forests (230 Mg/ha), with leaf area and average monthly temperature and rainfall being the most significant indicators of SOC.

- Li and others (2006) found continuous N addition in tropical soils of LEF significantly enhanced decay-resistant SOC (heavy-fraction organic carbon, HF-OC) sequestration, with a negligible effect on total SOC pool. More broadly, the study found N accumulation considerably increased aboveground leaf litter production and concentration while stimulating litter decay and fungal biomass growth (Li and others 2006).

Inceptisols from the cloud forest in El Yunque National Forest. (Photo by Maria M. Rivera)

- Despite the assumption that pasture-to-forest conversion will result in net carbon loss from soil, Silver and others (2004) found substantial net carbon sequestration in mature secondary lowland forest soils in the Cubuy Annex of the LEF.

- Based on drought responses of three study sites within the Bisley experimental watersheds, Wood and Silver (2012) found that decreased rainfall in humid tropical forests may cause a negative feedback to climate through lower soil CO_2 emission and higher CH_4 and N_2O soil consumption. They project future precipitation changes are likely to significantly affect the production and consumption of trace gases in soils.

- In wet tropical forests, hurricane-induced alterations of soil processes are significant. Given a doubling of major hurricane frequency to once every 25 years (Krishnamurti and others 1998), hurricane contribution to Puerto Rico's soil N_2O flux could increase to 30 percent of the period's total emissions (Erickson and Ayala 2004). Thus, future contributions of soil fluxes in Puerto Rico to the global N_2O budget are potentially great (Erickson and Ayala 2004).

- Together, N deposition and temperature alterations are likely to affect tropical soil CO_2 fluxes and carbon storage (Cusack and others 2012). Even small alterations in SOC storage may change the role of tropical forests as a carbon source or sink (Wang and others 2002).

- More intense and frequent droughts may favor species that are better able to allocate and store carbon to deep roots and lower soil horizons (Silver 1998).

- Fine root stocks are responsible for 30–70 percent of soil CO_2 flux (Schlesinger 1977) and are found by McGroddy and Silver (2000) to increase significantly with soil moisture. Fine root flux was positively correlated with total soil carbon content but negatively correlated with soil respiration rates, suggesting slower root turnover in wet soils.

- Greater precipitation quantity and frequency in dry tropical forests may cause more soil carbon to be stored aboveground, and will probably increase surface SOC pools (Silver 1998).

- Surface soil carbon pools in the wet tropical forest of Gulfo Dulce Forest Reserve, Costa Rica fluctuate respective to increases and decreases in litter inputs, whereas alterations in carbon inputs of temperate forest ecosystems are not as marked on carbon pools (Leff and others 2012).

Soil organisms

- Because of their high internal temperature optimum, thermo-tolerant bacterial community members dominate the warmer tropical soils (Balser and Wixon 2009). Though microbial soil processes will likely adjust to changes in rainfall, additional stressors of climate change may lower microorganism diversity or productivity, thus reducing microbial pool resiliency (Silver 1998).

Lianas growing in a moist forest in Costa Rica. (Photo by Paul Bolstad, University of Minnesota, Bugwood.org)

Vegetation Management

Carbon dynamics

- Silver and others (2004) identify the carbon sequestration potential of a 55-year-old reforested area within the Cubuy Annex of LEF to be significant in the later 33 years of growth, accumulating carbon (1.4 ± 0.05 Mg C/ha/year) at rates faster than documented in more mature, old-growth humid tropical forests. Similarly, Marín-Spiotta and others (2007) identify an 80-year-old patch of secondary forest in Sierra de Cayey, Puerto Rico with significant carbon sequestration rates in aboveground biomass.

- Climate change's ultimate effect on undisturbed tropical forest is a contended issue. On one side are those who argue that forests will continue to be net carbon sinks because of increased productivity via higher ambient CO_2 levels. On the other side are those who note that forests will be carbon sources because higher temperatures may increase plant and soil respiration and slow plant growth (Laurance and others 2011, Wood and others 2012) or because drought will lead to increased forest dieback (Allen and others 2010, McDowell and others 2011, Van Mantgem and others 2009).

- Meta-analyses of the effects of temperature on carbon storage and fluxes across a broad range of tropical forest sites have found that total NPP, litter production, tree growth, and belowground carbon allocation all increase with increasing mean annual temperature (Cleveland and others 2011, Raich and others 2006, Silver 1998) and temperature-to-precipitation ratio (Brown and Lugo 1982). However, soil carbon decomposition and turnover time also increase with increasing mean annual temperature, indicating that atmospheric carbon uptake via increased forest productivity could be offset by increased soil carbon loss with warming (Raich and others 2006).

- Numerous atmosphere-biosphere modeling studies suggest that warmer tropical forests will likely become an increasing source of carbon to the atmosphere from increased heterotrophic soil respiration (Cramer and others 2001), increased plant respiration (White and others 2000), decreased NPP or photosynthesis (Cramer and others 2001, White and others 2000), and/or forest dieback (White and others 2000).

- Eddy covariance data from the Brazilian Amazon combined with a simple gas-exchange model suggest that net ecosystem exchange is quite sensitive to temperature increases, and that the forest may switch from a carbon sink to a source with only a 1.2-°C increase in mean annual temperature (Grace and others 1996).

- A 1-year Amazonian eddy covariance dataset showed an overall trend of carbon source behavior at temperatures above about 27 °C (Doughty and Goulden 2008), and a 3-year dataset from a rain forest in Costa Rica showed reduced carbon sink behavior at air temperatures above 20 °C (Loescher and others 2003). A longer-term (4-year) eddy covariance study in the Amazon found the strongest controls of the components of net ecosystem exchange to be phenology and light rather than temperature (Hutyra and others 2007).

- Tian and others (1998) modeled the presence of a CO_2 "fertilization" effect which increased the net ecosystem production of undisturbed tropical ecosystems in the Amazon Basin from 1980 to 1994. They found plant growth to be directly stimulated by a net CO_2 gain of 3.3 Pg carbon and indirectly enhanced by greater plant water use efficiency. Silver (1998) contends that greater water use efficiency may result in increased soil moisture, potentially offsetting the drier soil expected from warmer and drier conditions.

- Terrestrial Ecosystem Models (TEMs) attribute year-to-year fluctuations in carbon storage and NPP potential to ENSO phase shifts and inter-annual temperature variations (Tian and others 1998). Thus, while normal wet and cool conditions make the Amazon Basin a net carbon sink, El Niño events induce drier and warmer weather, which decrease NPP and increase RH and make the Amazon a net carbon source in such years (Tian and others 1998).

- Chave and others (2008) found an overall increase in aboveground biomass among numerous old-growth forests throughout the tropics in recent decades.

Nutrient factors limiting productivity

- Higher temperatures could increase tropical soil organic matter decomposition rates, thus generally increasing soil nutrient availability and plant growth rates (Wood and others 2012). Conversely, additional nitrogen inputs may acidify the soil, deplete base cations, and activate aluminum ions, which when combined may decrease soil nutrient availability and plant growth rates (Lewis and others 2004). Furthermore, increased nutrient availability in response to rising temperatures could result in additional loss of nutrients to leaching if those nutrients are not rapidly utilized by the vegetation (Hedin and others 2003, Wood and others 2012).
- Current modeling efforts highlight the large role nutrient cycling could play in the response of the carbon cycle to climate change (e.g., Wang and Houlton 2009), and the few tropical fertilization studies that exist support this conclusion; however, how climate change will influence nutrient cycling in tropical forests remains largely unknown (Wood and others 2012).
- Nutrient availability has been shown to affect forest productivity and foliar nutrient concentrations, as well as rates of net photosynthesis and dark respiration (Cleveland and others 2011, Meir and others 2001, Wood and others 2009). Nutrient availability can also increase carbon loss to the atmosphere via positive effects on soil respiration and decomposition rates (Cleveland and Townsend 2006, Wood and Silver 2012).
- Wardle and others (2005) and McKane and others (1995) suggested that the availability of nutrients strongly limits productivity in highly weathered soils, such as those found in many tropical forests, and that forests on such soils have the potential to be more productive if their soils were more nutrient rich.
- Cleveland and others (2011) provide some evidence that soil phosphorus content and availability in moist and wet lowland tropical forests have both direct and indirect effects on the tropical carbon cycle.

Sierra palm (*Prestoea montana*) stand in El Yunque National Forest. (Photo by Whitney Cranshaw, Colorado State University, Bugwood.org)

Growth and yield

- Brandeis and others (2009), employing a cluster analysis of plot-level vegetation data from Puerto Rico and the U.S. Virgin Islands, found that vegetation assemblages in Puerto Rico are driven primarily by spring moisture stress but also by maximum and minimum temperatures, elevation, and distance from the coast.

- Long-term (five or more years) inventory plots in tropical forests around the globe have revealed contrasting trajectories of stand-level growth and biomass turnover. Datasets in tropical Africa and the Amazon have shown increasing growth rates (Lewis and others 2009b, Phillips and others 2004). Plots in Costa Rica, Panama, and Malaysia revealed decelerating growth (Clark and others 2003, Feeley and others 2007). A recent meta-analysis of large (16–52 ha), long-term tropical forest inventory plots across three continents (America, Africa, and Asia) showed an increase in biomass over 20 years in 7 of 10 plots analyzed (Chave and others 2008).
- Possible drivers of increasing biomass increment include: CO_2 fertilization (Lewis and others 2009a, Lloyd and Farquhar 2008); recovery from past disturbance (Chave and others 2008); or a shift in community composition towards faster growing species (Laurance and others 2004). Observed growth declines have been attributed to temperature-induced increases in plant respiration rates (Clark and others 2003, Feeley and others 2007, Wagner and others 2012); decreased net photosynthesis from increasing temperature beyond the thermal optimum (Doughty and Goulden 2008); or light limitation from increased liana shading of canopy trees or from global dimming (Feeley and others 2007).

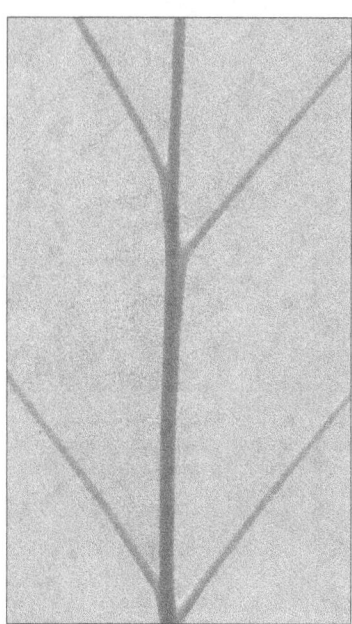

Leaf detail. (Photo by M. Solorzano)

Effects of temperature

- The ultimate physiological responses of tropical trees to climatic warming are still highly debated (Doughty and Goulden 2008, Lloyd and Farquhar 2008, Wood and others 2012), with some suggesting trees in the tropical lowlands are near a high temperature threshold (Doughty and Goulden 2008).

- Recent ex-situ studies suggest that the photosynthetic capacity of tropical plants may not be able to thermally acclimate to warming temperatures (Wood and others 2012). Leaf-level gas-exchange studies in Australia have shown that tropical species have lower photosynthetic thermal acclimation potential than temperate species, suggesting that tropical species may be more susceptible to climate change because they develop under lower seasonal and day-to-day temperature variation (Cunningham and Read 2002). In-situ experiments in the Amazon also showed no evidence of photosynthetic thermal acclimation in response to 13 weeks of 2 to 5 °C warming of existing leaves (Doughty 2011).

- It is unclear whether or not tropical plants will be able to thermally acclimate under naturally warming conditions, which occur more slowly than experimental warming conditions (Wood and others 2012).

- Cleveland and others (2011) found the mean annual temperature explained the largest amount of variance in aboveground NPP across moist and wet tropical forests types. However, after isolating the cool, upland forests with low NPP and the warm, lowland forests with higher NPP, the relationship became insignificant (Cleveland and others 2011).

- Recent studies suggest that increasing nighttime temperature may affect tropical tree growth and induce tree mortality (Clark and others 2010, Wagner and others 2012).

- Rain forest gap-phase regeneration will undergo slow changes in tandem with a warmer, more seasonal climate (Whitmore 1998).

- Warming may alter the morphology and biomass allocation patterns of trees in addition to affecting diameter growth rate (Wood and others 2012). A global meta-analysis of the effects of temperature on tree growth found warming increases foliage biomass, decreases root biomass, and produces taller, thinner stems, although tropical tree growth decreased overall when compared to either boreal or temperate species (Way and Oren 2010). In contrast, a study of tropical tree seedlings in Australia showed increased root-to-shoot ratios under warming treatments (Cunningham and Read 2003).

- Research on tropical rainforest species in Australia found that optimum growth occurred under temperatures that are much higher than is ideal for photosynthesis, indicating that growth can continue to increase with rising temperatures even as photosynthesis declines (Cunningham and Read 2003). The apparent disconnect between photosynthesis and growth showed that carbon source and sink activity could have more influence over a tree's growth rate than CO_2 exchange (Wood and others 2012).

Effects of rainfall (including temperature–moisture interactions)

- Increases in rainfall alone could raise NPP by increasing nutrient availability to the generally aerobic soil of the LEF lowland areas (Chacon and others 2006, Wang and others 2003, Wood and Silver 2012).

- In the LEF, Wang and others (2003) found that when holding all else constant, rainfall variation creates a small net increase in gross primary productivity (GPP) and NPP. Increasing only temperature, on the other hand, entails a much larger reduction in both GPP and NPP due to an increase in plant maintenance respiration and a decrease in stomatal conductance, with tabonuco-type forests being especially sensitive to temperature changes. The greatest negative effect to NPP and GPP was observed in a simulation of 11-percent less rainfall and a 2.5-°C higher temperature (Wang and others 2003).

- Wang and others (2003) utilized TEMs to simulate an increase in temperature and precipitation, which they found to greatly lower the NPP potential of the LEF. Melillo and others (1993) found similar results applying TEMs to a tropical evergreen forest.

- Water stress assessments for a generic crop at Adjuntas, Mayagüez, and Lajas, Puerto Rico yielded a 20-year average relative crop yield reduction that projected from 2000 to 2090 decreased water stress (from 12 to 6 percent) in the wet season and increased stress (from 51 to 64 percent) in the dry season (Harmsen and others 2009).

- Tropical rain forest seedlings will be affected by decreased rainfall, greater seasonality and variability, and lower soil moisture associated with climate change (Whitmore 1998).
- Where data have been combined globally, the sensitivity of rainforest tree mortality rates to soil moisture deficit (e.g., drought) appears to vary strongly by region, with the more humid rainforests of Southeast Asia showing substantially larger increases in mortality than those of Amazonia (Allen and others 2010, Phillips and others 2004).
- Hydraulic architecture may have a strong effect on how species react to global climate change. Trees with shallow roots may be at a competitive disadvantage compared to deeper rooted species (Stork and others 2007). In Amazonian forests, deep-rooted trees passively transfer water at night from deep moist soil to shallow dry soil, or from moist shallow to dry deep soil layers, a phenomenon called hydraulic redistribution (Oliveira and others 2005). If other tropical forest trees exhibit similar redistributive behaviors, the effects of increased evaporative demand with warming may be buffered for shallow-rooted species (Wood and others 2012).

Effects of elevated CO_2 concentrations
- Tabonuco forest species in the Luquillo Mountains experienced a much greater decrease in respiration and thus higher NPP than colorado, palm, or elfin forests under conditions of increased CO_2, temperature, and rainfall (Wang and others 2003).

- In their TEM simulation, Melillo and others (1993) found the direct effects of enriched CO_2 levels to be the most significant contributor to increases in NPP, as elevated CO_2 may decrease tree respiration rate.
- All else equal, lower stomatal conductance in response to higher CO_2 concentrations would increase water-use efficiency among tropical trees and could assist tree growth when water is a limiting factor (Lewis and others 2004).
- Among tropical plants, CO_2 has repeatedly been found to stimulate photosynthesis, accumulate more carbohydrates in plant tissue, and often deplete N reserves. However, tropical plant growth was found by Körner (2004) to be responsive to CO_2 only when there were abundant nutrients or deep shade and/or isolation.
- Early successional tropical tree species with high fertilization and relative growth rates are found to be more responsive to CO_2 (Körner 2004, Lewis and others 2004).
- Though CO_2-enhanced growth is expected to improve understory seedling survival and juvenile growth rates, young lianas may advance out of the forest shade and take greater advantage of the CO_2 enrichment. Such a biodiversity effect could shift the forest to earlier succession life stages and thus reduce the carbon-storing potential of the forest (Körner 2004, Lewis and others 2004).
- Recent or projected temperature increases may not decrease photosynthetic rates of tropical trees if the optimum temperature for photosynthesis rises and photorespiration declines with corresponding increases in CO_2 levels (Lewis and others 2004).

PR 191 provides access to El Yunque National Forest. (Photo by Lisa Jennings)

Effects on Social and Economic Resources

Recreation and Tourism

- Intensive land development, high coastal population density, and the effects of large tourism-based industry intensify the vulnerability of Puerto Rico to climatic variability, and there is limited human and capital infrastructure to address such problems (Lewsey and others 2004).

- Climate change may affect tourism through changes to local ecosystems and resources that impact scenic values; as well, changes to weather patterns may disrupt recreational activities, which can lead to changes in visitor use (Prideaux and others 2010).
- In wet tropical forests, the projected changes in forest structure and composition due to climate change are unlikely to result in noticeable changes in tourism demand; this is because most visitors have little knowledge of rainforest complexity and will not be able to observe these changes unless they are so extensive they cannot be ignored (Prideaux and others 2010). However, increased average high temperatures may affect demand due to visitor discomfort when recreating outdoors and an increased chance of heat-related illnesses (Prideaux and others 2010).
- Projected increases in disturbance events may lead to reduced tourist access in natural areas in an effort to protect public safety following events such as fire, insect outbreaks, blowdowns, and flooding. Extreme weather events may increase damage to facilities and structures and increase the need for road repairs (Joyce and others 2008).
- Climate change may lead to the redistribution of climatic aspects in tourist regions, which can affect tourism seasonality (e.g., changes in the length of the warm-weather tourism season), demand (e.g., increased destination choice in the winter), and travel patterns (e.g., changes in travel timing and destination). The Caribbean region, where year-round warm weather is the principle tourism resource, may see increasing competition from other regions as warm seasons expand globally (Scott and others 2004).
- In tropical coastal areas, negative effects of climate change through coral reef bleaching and sea level rise effects on beaches could affect economies that are dependent on tourism (Uyarra and others 2005). In a survey of tourists in Bonaire and Barbados, Uyarra and others (2005) found that 80 percent of tourists were unwilling to revisit the islands if coral reef bleaching and beach loss occur, unless they were able to pay a lower price.
- A study of beach-front resorts in the Caribbean found that with as little as 1-m sea level rise, 29 percent of properties would be partially or fully flooded, while 50–60 percent of properties would experience erosion damage (Scott and others 2012).

Land Use and Planning

Urban interactions
- According to data retrieved from the San Juan ATLAS Mission, the San Juan Metropolitan Area has greater sensible heat receptivity and therefore produces higher air temperatures (2.5 to 3 °C) (Comarazamy and others 2010).
- Additional urban and natural simulations showed bands of clouds and minimal precipitation in southwest San Juan Metropolitan Area, which may be due to less intense northeasterly trade winds transporting less available moisture horizontally (Comarazamy and others 2010).
- Results from eight urban and suburban forests in the Urban Long Term Research Area of Rio Piedras, Puerto Rico suggest that urbanization can alter ecosystem processes, microbial activity, and soil organic matter cycling, with a potential for a positive urban effect on soil mineral N pools in N-rich tropical forests (Cusack 2013).

- Comparing an old growth forested site to a nearby deforested grassland site near Sebana Seca, Puerto Rico, Van der Molen and others (2010) found that anthropogenic creation of pasture increased albedo and significantly lowered cloud condensate levels when compared to forest land, leading to a lower cloud base and reduced precipitation.

- Improved road conditions due to longer dry seasons are likely to influence land use decisions; for example, colonization and logging of the remaining "remote" forest may become more economically feasible, thus reducing tropical forest biodiversity in exchange for economic exploitation (Brodie and others 2011).
- Tropical land-cover change, resulting from direct human activities, interacts with anthropogenic ecosystem drivers such as climate change and affects watershed supply (Uriarte and others 2011).

Visitors to El Portal Rain Forest Center in El Yunque National Forest. (Photo by Maria M. Rivera)

- Urbanized landscapes can further exacerbate climate warming at the local scale, while highly vegetated tropical forests can have a moderate cooling effect (Lim and others 2005).

Energy production

- The climatological minimum wind blow—both current and future—is 4.84 m/s for the entire Caribbean region; therefore, this region can use advanced wind turbine technology to harness energy, perhaps enough to become self-sufficient. Wind energy, with small seasonal future variation, is particularly viable in both the dry season and early rainfall season, where wind power potential reaches at least Class 4 in Puerto Rico and the Lesser Antilles (Angeles 2010).

- The Caribbean region is expected to continue to have high solar energy availability in the future (currently, values are > 5.5 kWh/m^2 per day), making it an excellent candidate for sourcing renewable energy (Angeles and others 2007). Particularly, the southwest Caribbean is the highest net surface solar energy source, with dry season values ranging from 4 to 7 kWh/m^2 per day (Angeles and others 2007).

Urban forests in the San Juan Metropolitan Area. (Photo by Lisa Jennings)

Coastal Resources

Sea level rise trends

- Based on monthly averages from 1962 to 2006 (NOAA 2013), mean sea levels in San Juan, Puerto Rico have risen at a pace of 1.65 mm/year (± 0.52 mm/year).

- Average global sea level rise over the 20th century occurred at an average rate of 1.7 mm/year, with recent accelerations to 3.1 mm/year since the mid-1990s (Biasutti and others 2012, Church and White 2006). In the Caribbean specifically, sea levels have risen at a rate of about 1 mm/year over the 20th century (Cashman and others 2010).
- The IPCC Fourth Assessment Report projected with very high confidence (> 90 percent chance) a global rise in sea levels of at least 0.2 m by 2100, with high end projections of a 2-m rise in sea levels by 2100 (Parris and others 2012).
- Projections using the upcoming fifth edition of the IPCC assessment report estimate a global rise in sea levels of 0.57–1.10 m by 2100 (Jevrejeva and others 2012). However, this rise in sea level will not be uniform; sea levels in the Caribbean and Atlantic are projected to be as much as 5-cm higher than the global average (Galindo and others 2010).

Sea level rise effects

- In Sabana Seca on the northern coast of Puerto Rico, a study by Rivera-Ocasio and others (2007) found that small increases in salinity due to sea level rise could have substantial effects on coastal bloodwood (*Pterocarpus officinalis*) forests. Mangrove forests in the Caribbean region were also found to be vulnerable to sea level rise, as well as increased temperatures and hurricane frequency (Magrin and others 2007).

The beach in Piñones, Puerto Rico. (Photo by Lisa Jennings)

- In small (e.g., Antigua and Barbuda) and large (e.g., Puerto Rico) island states, sea level rise will cause a loss of land area, which could potentially lead to coastal erosion and loss of infrastructure as well as inland migrations of populations (Kelman and West 2009, Lewsey and others 2004).

- Urbanization throughout the Caribbean, created from the combination of tourism growth and deficient land-use planning and development controls, has rendered coastal infrastructure vulnerable to extreme weather and rising sea levels characteristic of climate change (Lewsey and others 2004).

- Saltwater intrusion into coastal aquifers due to sea level rise is already a threat to freshwater supplies in many Caribbean islands, and saltwater intrusion in the Caribbean is projected to increase with climate change (Cashman and others 2010, Lewsey and others 2004).

- Sea level rise, worsened by tropical storms, risks turning dynamic tropical wetland areas into salt pans, which may affect the colonization of some tropical birds (Şekercioğlu and others 2012).

Knowledge Gaps and Uncertainties

Knowledge of observed and projected climate change is continually evolving as scientists research the mechanisms and responses of the Earth's climate system to increased levels of CO_2 (IPCC 2001, 2007, 2013). In tropical and subtropical forests in particular, significant knowledge gaps exist in predicting the response of natural systems to climate change. There is a lack of large-scale manipulative experiments exposing species to warming and elevated CO_2 in the tropics and subtropics, and these studies are critical to understanding whether responses to climate change will be positive or negative (Zhou and others 2013). In addition, regionally downscaled climate models projecting temperature and precipitation patterns at fine scales are not readily available for locations within the Caribbean region, including Puerto Rico.[2] While existing large-scale global climate models are useful in determining potential future trends (Angeles and others 2007), the lack of fine-scale data in Puerto Rico's mountainous regions is especially troublesome as variations in climate with elevation over short horizontal distances cannot be captured by existing climate models (Meehl and others 2007), especially in predictions of extreme events (ECLAC 2010). Because of the lack of high-resolution climate projections, there are also few models representing potential implications of climate change for ecosystem functions and characteristics in the Caribbean region (see footnote 2). Natural resource managers and planners can look to studies of measured historical trends, as well as past periods of extreme climate events and the response of species to stress, to help forecast future responses (Walther and others 2002), as are presented in this report alongside future projections. However, knowledge gaps remain in the research of both historical responses and future trends for local ecosystems in the tropics and subtropics, and only a small number of the total plant and animal species in the region have been studied. While this section points out several examples of research needs, a broader assessment of knowledge gaps related to climate change in EYNF, Puerto Rico, and the Caribbean region is needed.

Uncertainties exist with any study forecasting trends in climate. The scientific literature assessed here employs various measures of uncertainty related to specific effects of climate change. While it is impractical to describe each measure of uncertainty here, it is important to understand the inherent uncertainties in the broader discussion of climate change. The IPCC provides an overview of key uncertainties in both historic observations and projections of climate change in its most recent Fifth Assessment Report (IPCC 2013) to help readers understand the uncertainties surrounding drivers and effects of climate change. The IPCC relates the probability of changes to terms describing likelihood using the following metrics: certain (100 percent probability), virtually certain (99–100 percent), very likely (90–100 percent), likely (66–100 percent), about as likely as not (33–66 percent), unlikely (0–33 percent), very unlikely (0–10 percent), and exceptionally unlikely (0–1 percent). Key measures of uncertainty from the IPCC (2013) related to projected future conditions described in this report are:

- Globally, climate warming since the 1950s is certain, and it is likely that the 30-year period from 1983 to 2012 was the warmest period in the last 1,400 years. It is virtually certain that temperatures will continue to increase through the late 21st century.
- It is very likely that climate change has contributed to a global increase in the frequency and intensity of temperature extremes. It is virtually certain that these events will become more frequent through the late 21st century.

---

[2] Personal communication. 2013. K. Cepero, Research Assistant, North Carolina State University, Campus Box 7260, Raleigh, NC 27606.

- It is likely that climate change has influenced global precipitation patterns since the 1960s, including the intensification of both drought and heavy precipitation events. It is very likely these events will become more frequent and/or intense through the late 21st century.
- It is virtually certain that there has been an increase in intense hurricanes in the north Atlantic Ocean since the 1970s. It is more likely than not that these events will continue to increase in intensity through the late 21st century.
- It is virtually certain that sea surface temperatures have warmed since the 1970s. It is certain that sea levels are rising, and it is likely that the rate of sea level rise has accelerated over the 20th century. It is virtually certain that sea levels will continue to rise through the late 21st century.

It is important to note that the uncertainties presented here are not comprehensive. More detailed information can be found in the IPCC Fifth Assessment Report (IPCC 2013).

Acknowledgments

Content in this document was produced by the development team for the USDA Forest Service TACCIMO tool in conjunction with the IITF and managers at EYNF. This work was supported by the USDA Forest Service Eastern Forest Environmental Threat Assessment Center (EFETAC) cooperative agreements 11-CR-11330147-016 and 12-CS-11330147-113 funded through North Carolina State University, and grant DEB 1239764 from the National Science Foundation to the Institute for Tropical Ecosystem Studies, University of Puerto Rico, and the IITF, as part of the Luquillo Long Term Ecological Research Program. Federal staff support was provided by the USDA Forest Service Southern Research Station, EFETAC, IITF, and the Southern Region (Region 8) of the National Forest System.

Strategic planning—Visioning and key management direction was provided by Pedro Rios, Ecosystem Management and Forest Planning Team Leader, EYNF. David Meriwether, Ecosystem Management Coordinator, USDA Forest Service Southern Region, and Steven McNulty, Landscape Ecologist, EFETAC, are acknowledged for their role in strategic planning of the regional response to climate change under the alternative planning rule (USDA Forest Service 2012).

Content development—Access to and review of information within the IITF library was provided by Gisel Reyes, Technical Information Specialist, and Julie Hernández, Clerk. Keren Cepero, Ph.D. candidate, North Carolina State University, is acknowledged for her contributions to geospatial products. The EFETAC TACCIMO development team— including Steven McNulty; Jennifer Moore Myers, Resource Information Specialist; and Robert Herring, IT Specialist—is acknowledged for its role in the development of the TACCIMO framework.

Review and comments—The interdisciplinary team for the EYNF Land and Resource Management Plan revision is acknowledged for contributing reviews and comments on TACCIMO products. Ariel Lugo, Frank Wadsworth, Joseph Wunderle, Jennifer Moore Myers, Kathleen McGinley, Luis Rivera, Peter Weaver, Steven McNulty, Tamara Heartsill-Scalley, Tana Wood, Tinelle Bustam, Wayne Arendt, William Gould, and William McDowell are acknowledged for their thoughtful reviews of this report.

Literature Cited

Addo-Bediako, A.S.; Chown, S.; Gaston, K.J. 2000. Thermal tolerance, climatic variability and latitude. Proceedings of the Royal Society of London. Series B: Biological Sciences. 267(1445): 739-745.

Aguilar, E.; Peterson, T.C.; Obando, P.R. [and others]. 2005. Changes in precipitation and temperature extremes in Central America and northern South America, 1961–2003. Journal of Geophysical Research. 110(D23): D23107. doi: 10.1029/2005JD006119. [Date accessed: January 27, 2012].

Allen, C.D.; Macalady, A.K.; Chenchouni, H. [and others]. 2010. A global overview of drought and heat-induced tree mortality reveals emerging climate change risks for forests. Forest Ecology and Management. 259(4): 660-684.

Anchukaitis, K. J.; Evans, M.N. 2010. Tropical cloud forest climate variability and the demise of the Monteverde golden toad. Proceedings of the National Academy of Sciences. 107(11): 5036-5040.

Anderson, B. 2011. Near-term increase in frequency of seasonal temperature extremes prior to the 2 C global warming target. Climatic Change. 108(3): 581-589.

Angeles, M.E ; González, J.E.; Erickson, D.J.; Hernández, J.L. 2007. Predictions of future climate change in the Caribbean region using global general circulation models. International Journal of Climatology. 27(5): 555-569.

Angeles, M.E ; González, J.E.; Erickson, D.J.; Hernández, J.L. 2010. The impacts of climate changes on the renewable energy resources in the Caribbean region. Journal of Solar Energy Engineering. 132(3): 031009. doi:10 1115/1.4001475. [Date accessed: August 2, 2012].

Angulo-Sandoval, P.; Fernández-Marín, H.; Zimmerman, J.K.; Alde, T.M. 2004. Changes in patterns of understory leaf phenology and herbivory following hurricane damage. Biotropica. 36(1): 60-67.

Arendt, W. J. 2000. Impact of nest predators, competitors, and ectoparasites on pearly-eyed thrashers, with comments on the potential implications for Puerto Rican parrot recovery. Ornitología Neotropical. 11: 13-63.

Arendt, W.J. 2006. Adaptations of an avian supertramp: distribution, ecology, and life history of the pearly-eyed thrasher (*Margarops fuscatus*). Gen Tech. Rep. IITF-GTR-27. U.S. Department of Agriculture Forest Service, International Institute of Tropical Forestry. 154 p. http://www.fs.fed.us/global/iitf/pubs/iitf-gtr27a.pdf. [Date accessed: June 18, 2013].

Balser, T.C.; Wixon, D.L. 2009. Investigating biological control over soil carbon temperature sensitivity. Global Change Biology. 15(12): 2935-2949.

Barker, B.S ; Waide, R.B.; Cook, J.A. 2011. Deep intra-island divergence of a montane forest endemic: phylogeography of the Puerto Rican frog (*Eleutherodactylus portoricensis*) (anura: Eleutherodactylidae). Journal of Biogeography. 38(12): 2311-2325.

Barone, J.A.; Thomlinson, J.; Cordero, P.A ; Zimmerman, J.K. 2008. Metacommunity structure of tropical forest along an elevation gradient in Puerto Rico. Journal of Tropical Ecology. 24(5): 525-534.

Bedsworth, L. 2012. Air quality planning in California's changing climate. Climatic Change. 111(1): 101-118.

Benzing, D.H. 1998. Vulnerabilities of tropical forests to climate change: the significance of resident epiphytes. Climatic Change. 39(2): 519-540.

Biasutti, M ; Sobel, A.H.; Camargo, S.J.; Creyts, T.T. 2012. Projected changes in the physical climate of the Gulf Coast and Caribbean. Climatic Change. 112(3-4): 819-845.

Blaustein, A.R.; Belden, L.K.; Olson, D.H. [and others]. 2001. Amphibian breeding and climate change. Conservation Biology. 15(6): 1804-1809.

Blaustein, A.R.; Walls, S.C ; Bancroft, B.A. [and others]. 2010. Direct and indirect effects of climate change on amphibian populations. Diversity. 2(2): 281-313.

Bloch, C.P.; Willig, M.R. 2006. Context-dependence of long-term responses of terrestrial gastropod populations to large-scale disturbance. Journal of Tropical Ecology. 22(2): 111-122.

Blundell, A G.; Scatena, F.N ; Wentsel, R.; Sommers, W. 2003. Ecorisk assessment using indicators of sustainability: invasive species in the Caribbean National Forest of Puerto Rico. Journal of Forestry. 101(1): 14-19.

Bradshaw, C.J.A.; Giam, X.; Tan, H.T.W. [and others]. 2008. Threat or invasive status in legumes is related to opposite extremes of the same ecological and life-history attributes. Journal of Ecology. 96: 869–883.

Brandeis, T.J.; Helmer, E.H ; Marcano-Vega, H.; Lugo, A.E. 2009. Climate shapes the novel plant communities that form after deforestation in Puerto Rico and the U.S. Virgin Islands. Forest Ecology and Management. 258(7): 1704-1718.

Brandeis, T.J.; Woodall, C.W. 2008. Assessment of forest fuel loadings in Puerto Rico and the U.S. Virgin Islands. AMBIO: A Journal of the Human Environment. 37(7): 557-562.

Breshears, D.D.; Cobb, N.S.; Rich, P.M. [and others]. 2005. Regional vegetation die-off in response to global-change-type drought. Proceedings of the National Academy of Sciences. 102(42): 15,144-15,148.

Brodie, J.; Post, E.; Laurance, W.F. 2011. Climate change and tropical biodiversity: a new focus. Trends in Ecology and Evolution. 27(3): 1-6.

Brokaw, N.; Crowl, T.; Lugo, A. [and others]. 2012. A Caribbean forest tapestry: the multidimensional nature of disturbance and response. New York: Oxford University Press. 464 p.

Brown, S.; Lugo, A.E. 1982. The storage and production of organic-matter in tropical forests and their role in the global carbon cycle. Biotropica. 14: 161-187.

Bruijnzeel, L.A.; Mulligan, M.; Scatena, F.N. 2011. Hydrometeorology of tropical montane cloud forests: emerging patterns. Hydrological Processes. 25(3): 465-498.

Burney, D.A.; Burney, L.P.; MacPhee, R.D.E. 1994. Holocene charcoal stratigraphy from Laguna Tortuguero, Puerto Rico, and the timing of human arrival on the island. Journal of Archaeological Science. 21: 273-281.

Burrowes, P.A.; Joglar, R.L.; Green, D.E. 2004. Potential causes for amphibian declines in Puerto Rico. Herpetologica. 60(2): 141-154.

Bytnerowicz, A.; Omasa, K.; Paoletti, E. 2007. Integrated effects of air pollution and climate change on forests: a northern hemisphere perspective. Environmental Pollution. 147: 438-445.

Campbell, J.D.; Taylor, M.A.; Stephenson, T.S. [and others]. 2011. Future climate of the Caribbean from a regional climate model. International Journal of Climatology. 31(12): 1866-1878.

Carey, C.; Heyer, W.R.; Wilkinson, J. [and others]. 2001. Amphibian declines and environmental change: use of remote-sensing data to identify environmental correlates. Conservation Biology. 15(4): 903-913.

Carpenter, S.R.; Fisher, S.G.; Grimm, N.B.; Kitchell, J.F. 1992. Global change and freshwater ecosystems. Annual Review Ecological Systems. 23: 119-139.

Cashman, A.; Nurse, L.; John, C. 2010. Climate change in the Caribbean: the water management implications. The Journal of Environment Development. 19(1): 42-67.

Chacon, N.; Silver, W.; Dubinsky, E.; Cusack, D. 2006. Iron reduction and soil phosphorus solubilization in humid tropical forests soils: the roles of labile carbon pools and an electron shuttle compound. Biogeochemistry. 78: 67-84.

Chave, J.; Condit, R.; Muller-Landau, H.C. [and others]. 2008. Assessing evidence for a pervasive alteration in tropical tree communities. PLoS Biology. 6(3): e45. doi:10.1371/journal.pbio.0060045. [Date accessed: July 16, 2012].

Chaves, L.F.; Morrison, A.C.; Kitron, U.D.; Scott, T.W. 2012. Nonlinear impacts of climatic variability on the density-dependent regulation of an insect vector of disease. Global Change Biology. 18(2): 457-468.

Chazdon, R.L.; Brenes, A.R.; Alvarado, B.V. 2005. Effects of climate and stand age on annual tree dynamics in tropical second-growth rain forests. Ecology. 86: 1808-1815.

Chen, I.C.; Shiu, H.J.; Benedick, S. [and others]. 2009. Elevation increases in moth assemblages over 42 years on a tropical mountain. Proceedings of the National Academy of Sciences. 106(5): 1479-1483.

Christensen, J.H.; Hewitson, B.; Busuioc, A. [and others]. 2007. Regional climate projections. In: Solomon, S.; Qin, D.; Manning, M.; comps., eds. Climate Change 2007: The Physical Science Basis. Contribution of Working Group I to the Fourth Assessment Report of the Intergovernmental Panel on Climate Change. Cambridge, United Kingdom and New York, USA: Cambridge University Press: 892-896.

Church, J.; White, N. 2006. A 20th century acceleration in global sea-level rise. Geophysical Research Letters. 33(1): L01602. doi:10.1029/2005GL024826. [Date accessed: September 8, 2011].

Clark D.B.; Clark D.A.; Oberbauer S.F. 2010. Annual wood production in a tropical rain forest in NE Costa Rica linked to climatic variation but not to increasing CO_2. Global Change Biology. 16: 747–759.

Clark, D.A.; Piper, S.C.; Keeling, C.D.; Clark, D.B. 2003. Tropical rain forest tree growth and atmospheric carbon dynamics linked to interannual temperature variation during 1984–2000. Proceedings of the National Academy of Sciences. 100(10): 5852-5857.

Cleveland, C.C.; Townsend, A.R. 2006. Nutrient additions to a tropical rain forest drive substantial soil carbon dioxide losses to the atmosphere. Proceedings of the National Academy of Sciences. 103(27): 10,316-10,321.

Cleveland, C.C.; Townsend, A.R.; Taylor, P. [and others]. 2011. Relationships among net primary productivity, nutrients and climate in tropical rain forest: a pan-tropical analysis. Ecology Letters. 14(9): 939-947.

Cochrane, M.A.; Laurance, W.F. 2008. Synergisms among fire, land use, and climate change in the Amazon. AMBIO: A Journal of the Human Environment. 37(7): 522-527.

Comarazamy, D.E ; González, J.E. 2011. Regional long-term climate change (1950–2000) in the midtropical Atlantic and its impacts on the hydrological cycle of Puerto Rico. Journal of Geophysical Research. 116(D21): D00Q05. doi:10.1029/2010JD015414. [Date accessed: July 16, 2012].

Comarazamy, D.E ; González, J.E.; Luvall, J.C. [and others]. 2010. A land-atmospheric interaction study in the coastal tropical city of San Juan, Puerto Rico. Earth Interactions. 14(16): 1-24.

Covich, A.P.; Crowl, T.A.; Heartsill-Scalley, T. 2006. Effects of drought and hurricane disturbances on headwater distributions of palaemonid river shrimp (*Macrobrachium* spp.) in the Luquillo Mountains, Puerto Rico. 2006. Journal of the North American Benthological Society. 25(1): 99-107.

Covich, A.P.; Crowl, T.A.; Scatena, F.N. 2003. Effects of extreme low flows on freshwater shrimps in a perennial tropical stream. Freshwater Biology. 48(7): 1199-1206.

Cramer, W.; Bondeau, A.; Woodward, F.I. [and others]. 2001. Global response of terrestrial ecosystem structure and function to CO_2 and climate change: results from six dynamic global vegetation models. Global Change Biology. 7(4): 357-373.

Crick, H.Q.P. 2004. The impact of climate change on birds. Ibis. 146(s1): 48-56.

Crook, K.E.; Pringle, C.M.; Freeman, M.C. 2009. A method to assess longitudinal riverine connectivity in tropical streams dominated by migratory biota. Aquatic Conservation: Marine and Freshwater Ecosystems. 19(6): 714-723.

Crook, K.E.; Scatena, F.N ; Pringle, C.M. 2007. Water withdrawn from the Luquillo Experimental Forest, 2004. Gen. Tech. Rep. IITF-GTR-34. San Juan, Puerto Rico: U.S. Department of Agriculture Forest Service, International Institute of Tropical Forestry. 26 p.

Cunningham, S.C.; Read, J. 2002. Do temperate rainforest trees have a greater ability to acclimate to changing temperatures than tropical rainforest trees? New Phytologist. 157(1): 55-64.

Cunningham, S.C.; Read, J. 2003. Comparison of temperate and tropical rainforest tree species: growth responses to temperature. Journal of Biogeography. 30(1): 143-153.

Cusack, D.F. 2013. Soil nitrogen levels are linked to decomposition enzyme activities along an urban-remote tropical forest gradient. Soil Biology and Biochemistry. 57: 192-203.

Cusack, D.F ; Silver, W.L.; Torn, M.S. [and others]. 2011. Changes in microbial community characteristics and soil organic matter with nitrogen additions in two tropical forests. Ecology. 92(3): 621-632.

Cusack, D.F ; Torn, M.S.; McDowell, W.H.; Silver, W.L. 2012. The response of heterotrophic activity and carbon cycling to nitrogen additions and warming in two tropical soils. Global Change Biology. 18(1): 400.

Daly, C.; Helmer, E.H.; Quiñones, M. 2003. Mapping the climate of Puerto Rico, Vieques, and Culebra. International Journal of Climatology. 23: 1359-1381.

Dawson, W.R.; O'Connor, T.P. 1996. Energetic features of avian thermoregulatory responses. In: Carey, C., ed. Avian energetics and nutritional ecology. New York: Chapman and Hall: 85-124.

Deutsch, C.A.; Tewksbury, J.J.; Huey, R.B. [and others]. 2008. Impacts of climate warming on terrestrial ectotherms across latitude. Proceedings of the National Academy of Sciences. 105 (18): 6668-6672.

Diffenbaugh, N.; Scherer, M. 2011. Observational and model evidence of global emergence of permanent, unprecedented heat in the 20th and 21st centuries. Climatic Change. 107(3-4): 615-624.

Dillon, M.E.; Wang, G.; Huey, R.B. 2010. Global metabolic impacts of recent climate warming. Nature. 467: 704-707.

Donnelly, M.A.; Crump, M.L. 1998. Potential effects of climate change on two neotropical amphibian assemblages. Climatic Change. 39(2): 541-561.

Doughty, C E. 2011. An in situ leaf and branch warming experiment in the Amazon. Biotropica. 43(6): 658-665.

Doughty, C E.; Goulden, M.L. 2008. Are tropical forests near a high temperature threshold? Journal of Geophysical Research. 113(G1): G00B07. doi:10.1029/2007JG000632. [Date accessed: August 10, 2012].

Doyle, T.W. 1981. The role of disturbance in gap dynamics of a montane rain forest: an application of a tropical succession model. In: West D.C ; Shugart H.H.; Botkin D.B., eds. Forest succession concepts and applications. New York: Springer Verlag, 56-73.

Dugger, K.M.; Faaborg, J.; Arendt, E.J.; Hobson, K.A. 2004. Understanding survival and abundance of overwintering warblers: does rainfall matter? The Condor. 106(4): 744-760.

Dukes, J.S.; Pontius, J.; Orwig, D. [and others]. 2008. Responses of insect pests, pathogens, and invasive plant species to climate change in the forests of Northeastern North America: what can we predict? Canadian Journal of Forest Research. 39(2): 231-248.

Economic Commission for Latin America and the Caribbean (ECLAC). 2010. Regional climate modeling in the Caribbean. 28 p. http://www.eclac.org/publicaciones/xml/2/39862/LCARL.265.pdf. [Date accessed: November 4, 2013].

Emmanuel, K.A. 1987. The dependence of hurricane intensity on Climate. Nature. 326: 483-485.

Erickson, H.E.; Ayala, G. 2004. Hurricane-induced nitrous oxide fluxes from a wet tropical forest. Global Change Biology. 10(7): 1155-1162.

Eugster, W.; Burkard, R.; Holwerda, F. [and others]. 2006. Characteristics of fog and fogwater fluxes in a Puerto Rican elfin cloud forest. Agricultural and Forest Meteorology. 139(3-4): 288-306.

Faaborg, J.; Arendt, W.J.; Toms, J.D. [and others]. 2013. Long-term decline of a winter-resident bird community in Puerto Rico. Biodiversity and Conservation. 22(1): 63-75.

Feeley, K. J.; Joseph Wright, S.; Supardi, N. [and others]. 2007. Decelerating growth in tropical forest trees. Ecology Letters. 10(6): 461-469.

Ferreira de Siqueira, M.; Peterson, A.T. 2003. Global climate change consequences for Cerrado tree species. Biota Neotropica. 3: 1-14.

Ficke, A.D.; Myrick, C.A.; Hansen, L.J. 2007. Potential impacts of global climate change on freshwater fisheries. Reviews in Fish Biology and Fisheries. 17(4): 581-613.

Flannigan, M.D.; Stocks, B.J ; Wotton, B.M. 2000. Climate change and forest fires. Science of the Total Environment. 262: 221-229.

Fraser, K.C ; Kyser, T.K.; Ratcliffe, L.M. 2008. Detecting altitudinal migration events in neotropical birds using stable isotopes. Biotropica. 40(3): 269-272.

Galindo, L.M.; de Miguel, C ; Ferrer, J. 2010. Vital climate change graphics for Latin America and the Caribbean. Panama City, Panama: The United National Environmental Programme. http://www.pnuma.org/english/comunicados/061210/LAC_Web_eng_2010-12-07.pdf. [Date accessed: June 18, 2013].

Gioda, A ; Mayol-Bracero, O.L.; Scatena, F.N. [and others]. 2013. Chemical constituents in clouds and rainwater in the Puerto Rican rainforest: potential sources and seasonal drivers. Atmospheric Environment. 68: 208-220.

Girvetz, E.H.; Zganjar, C.; Raber, G.T. [and others]. 2009. Applied climate-change analysis: the Climate Wizard tool. PLoS ONE. 4 (12): e8320. doi:10.1371/journal.pone.0008320. [Date accessed: December 14, 2012].

Godley B.J.; Broderick A.C ; Downie J.R. 2001. Thermal conditions in nests of loggerhead turtles: further evidence suggesting female skewed sex ratios of hatchling production in the Mediterranean. Journal of Experimental Marine Biology and Ecology. 263: 45-63.

González, G.; Waide, R.B; Willig, M.R. 2013a. Advancements in the understanding of spatiotemporal gradients in tropical landscapes: a Luquillo focus and global perspective. Ecological Bulletins. 54: 245-250.

González, G.; Willig, M.R.; Waide, R.B. 2013b. Ecological gradient analysis in a tropical landscape: multiples perspectives and emerging themes. Ecological Bulletins. 54: 13-20.

Gould, W.A ; González, G.; Hudak, A.T. [and others]. 2008. Forest structure and downed woody debris in boreal, temperate, and tropical forest fragments. AMBIO: A Journal of the Human Environment. 37(7/8): 577-587.

Grace, J.; Malhi, Y.; Lloyd, J. [and others]. 1996. The use of eddy covariance to infer the net carbon dioxide uptake of Brazilian rain forest. Global Change Biology. 2(3): 209-217.

Granados, J.; Körner, C. 2002. In deep shade, elevated CO_2 increases the vigor of tropical climbing plants. Global Change Biology. 8: 1109-1117.

Guariguata, M.R.; Cornelius, J.P.; Locatelli, B. [and others]. 2008. Mitigation needs adaptation: tropical forestry and climate change. Mitigation and Adaptation Strategies for Global Change. 13(8): 793-808.

Gunderson, A.R.; Leal, M. 2012. Geographic variation in vulnerability to climate warming in a tropical Caribbean lizard. Functional Ecology. 26(4): 783-793.

Gunderson, A.R.; Siegel, J.; Leal, M. 2011. Tests of the contribution of acclimation to geographic variation in water loss rates of the West Indian lizard (*Anolis cristatellus*). Journal of Comparative Physiology B: Biochemical, Systemic, and Environmental Physiology. 181(7): 965-972.

Hannah, L.; Betts, R.A.; Shugart, H.H. 2011. Modeling future effects of climate change on tropical forests. In: Bush, M.B.; Flenley, J.R.; Gosling, W.D., eds. Tropical Rainforest Responses to Climatic Change. Heidelberg: Springer-Verlag: 411-429.

Hannah, L.; Lovejoy, T. 2011. Conservation, climate change, and tropical forests. In: Bush, M.B.; Flenley, J.R.; Gosling, W.D., eds. Tropical Rainforest Responses to Climatic Change. Heidelberg: Springer-Verlag: 431-443.

Harmsen, E.W.; Miller, N.L.; Schlegel, N.J ; Gonzalez, J.E. 2009. Seasonal climate change impacts on evapotranspiration, precipitation deficit and crop yield in Puerto Rico. Agricultural Water Management. 96(7): 1085-1095.

Hawkes L.A.; Broderick A.C ; Godfrey M.H.; Godley B.J. 2009. Climate change and marine turtles. Endangered Species Research. 7: 137-154.

Heartsill-Scalley, T ; Scatena, F.N.; Estrada, C. [and others]. 2007. Disturbance and long-term patterns of rainfall and throughfall nutrient fluxes in a subtropical wet forest in Puerto Rico. Journal of Hydrology. 333(2-4): 472-485.

Heartsill-Scalley, T ; Scatena, F.N.; Lugo, A.E. [and others]. 2010. Changes in structure, composition, and nutrients during 15 years of hurricane-induced succession in a subtropical wet forest in Puerto Rico. Biotropica. 42(4): 455-463.

Hedin, L.O.; Vitousek, P.M.; Matson, P.A. 2003. Nutrient losses over four million years of tropical forest development. Ecology. 84: 2231–2255.

Hellmann, J.J.; Byers, J.E ; Bierwagen, B.G.; Dukes, J.S. 2008. Five potential consequences of climate change for invasive species. Conservation Biology. 22(3): 534-543.

Hertz, P.E.; Arce-Hernandez, A ; Ramirez-Vazquez, J.W. [and others]. 1979. Geographical variation of heat sensitivity and water loss rates in the tropical lizard, *Anolis gundlachi*. Comparative Biochemistry and Physiology Part A: Physiology. 62(4): 947-953.

Hillman S ; Gorman G.C.; Thomas R. 1979. Water loss in *Anolis* lizards: evidence for acclimation and intraspecific differences along a habitat gradient. Comparative Biochemistry and Physiology Part A: Physiology. 62(4): 491-494.

Holdridge, L.R. 1967. Life zone ecology. San Juan, Costa Rica: Tropical Science Center. 206 p.

Huey, R.B.; Deutsch, C.A.; Tewksbury, J.J. [and others]. 2009. Why tropical forest lizards are vulnerable to climate warming. Proceedings of the Royal Society B: Biological Sciences. 276(1664): 1939-1948.

Hughes, L.; Cawsey, E.M.; Westoby, M. 1996. Climatic range sizes of *Eucalyptus* species in relation to future climate change. Global Ecology and Biogeography Letters. 5: 23-29.

Hutyra, L.R.; Munger, J.W.; Saleska, S.R. [and others]. 2007. Seasonal controls on the exchange of carbon and water in an Amazonian rain forest. Journal of Geophysical Research. 112(G3): G03008. doi:10 1029/2006JG000365.

Intergovernmental Panel on Climate Change (IPCC). 2001. Climate change 2001: synthesis report. In: Watson, R.T., ed. A Contribution of Working Groups I, II and III to the Third Assessment Report of the Intergovernmental Panel on Climate Change. Cambridge, UK: Cambridge University Press: 398 p.

IPCC. 2007. Climate change 2007: synthesis report. In: Watson, R.T., ed. A Contribution of Working Groups I, II and III to the Fourth Assessment Report of the Intergovernmental Panel on Climate Change. Cambridge, UK: Cambridge University Press: 104 p.

IPCC. 2013. Climate change 2013: the physical science basis. In: Joussaume, S.; Penner, J.; and Tangang, F., eds. A Contribution of Working Group I to the Fifth Assessment Report of the Intergovernmental Panel on Climate Change. Cambridge, UK: Cambridge University Press: 2216 p.

Jevrejeva, S.; Moore, J.C.; Grinsted, A. 2012. Sea level projections to A.D. 2500 with a new generation of climate change scenarios. Global and Planetary Change. 80-81: 14-20.

Jones, G.; Jacobs, D.S.; Kunz, T.H. [and others]. 2009. Carpe noctem: the importance of bats as bioindicators. Endangered Species Research. 8(1-2): 93-115.

Joyce, L.A.; Blate, G.M.; Littell, J.S. [and others]. 2008. National forests. In: Julius, S. H ; West, J.M., eds. Preliminary review of adaptation options for climate-sensitive ecosystems and resources. Washington, DC: U.S. Environmental Protection Agency: 3-1 to 3-127.

Karl, T.R ; Melillo, J.M ; Peterson, T.C. 2009. Global climate change impacts in the United States. New York: Cambridge University Press. 188 p.

Kelman, I ; West, J.J. 2009. Climate change and small island developing states: a critical review. Ecological and Environmental Anthropology. 5(1): 1-16.

Knutson, T.R ; McBride, J.L ; Chan, J. [and others]. 2010. Tropical cyclones and climate change. Nature Geoscience. 3(3): 157-163.

Koopowitz, H.; Hawkins, B.A. 2012. Global climate change is confounding species conservation strategies. Integrative Zoology. 7(2): 158-164.

Körner, C. 2004. Through enhanced tree dynamics carbon dioxide enrichment may cause tropical forests to lose carbon. Philosophical Transactions of the Royal Society of London, Series B: Biological Sciences. 359(1443): 493-498.

Krishnamurti T.N.; Correa-Torres R ; Latif, M. [and others]. 1998. The impact of current and possibly future sea surface temperature anomalies on the frequency of Atlantic hurricanes. Tellus A. 50(2): 186-210.

Larsen, M.C. 2000. Analysis of 20th century rainfall and streamflow to characterize drought and water resources in Puerto Rico. Physical Geography. 21(6): 494-521.

Lasso, E.; Ackerman, J.D. 2003. Flowering phenology of *Werauhia sintenisii*, a bromeliad from the dwarf montane forest in Puerto Rico: an indicator of climate change? Selbyana. 24(1): 95-104.

Lasso, E.; Ackerman, J.D. 2012. Nutrient limitation restricts growth and reproductive output in a tropical montane cloud forest bromeliad: findings from a long-term forest fertilization experiment. Oecologia. 171(1): 165-174.

Laurance, W.F.; Oliveira, A.A.; Laurance, S.G. [and others]. 2004. Pervasive alteration of tree communities in undisturbed Amazonian forests. Nature. 428(6979): 171-175.

Laurance, W.F.; Useche, D.C.; Shoo, L.P. [and others]. 2011. Global warming, elevational ranges and the vulnerability of tropical biota. Biological Conservation. 144(1): 548-557.

LaVal, R.K. 2004. Impact of global warming and locally changing climate on tropical cloud forest bats. Journal of Mammalogy. 85(2): 237-244.

Leff, J.W.; Wieder, W.R.; Taylor, P.G. [and others]. 2012. Experimental litterfall manipulation drives large and rapid changes in soil carbon cycling in a wet tropical forest. Global Change Biology. 18(9): 2969-2979.

Lewis, S.L. 2006. Tropical forests and the changing earth system. Philosophical Transactions of the Royal Society of London, Series B: Biological Sciences. 361(1465): 195-210.

Lewis, S.L.; Lloyd, J.; Sitch, S. [and others]. 2009a. Changing ecology of tropical forests: evidence and drivers. Annual review of Ecology, Evolution, and Systematics. 40: 529-549.

Lewis, S.L.; Lopez-Gonzalez, G.; Sonké, B. [and others]. 2009b. Increasing carbon storage in intact African tropical forests. Nature. 457(7232): 1003-1006.

Lewis, S.L.; Malhi, Y.; Phillips, O.L. 2004. Fingerprinting the impacts of global change on tropical forests. Philosophical Transactions of the Royal Society of London, Series B: Biological Sciences. 359(1443): 437-462.

Lewsey, C.; Cid, G.; Kruse, E. 2004. Assessing climate change impacts on coastal infrastructure in the eastern Caribbean. Marine Policy. 28(5): 393-409.

Li, Y.; Xu, M.; Zou, X. 2006. Effects of nutrient additions on ecosystem carbon cycle in a Puerto Rican tropical wet forest. Global Change Biology. 12(2): 284-293.

Lim, Y.K.; Cai, M.; Kalnay, E.; Zhou, L. 2005. Observational evidence of sensitivity of surface climate changes to land types and urbanization. Geophysical Research Letters. 32(22): L22712. doi: 10 1029/2005GL024267. [Date accessed: June 11, 2013].

Linkov, I.; Loney, D.; Cormier, S. [and others]. 2009. Weight-of-evidence evaluation in environmental assessment: review of qualitative and quantitative approaches. Science of the Total Environment. 407: 5199-5205.

Lintner, B.R.; Biasutti, M.; Diffenbaugh, N.S. [and others]. 2012. Amplification of wet and dry month occurrence over tropical land regions in response to global warming. Journal of Geophysical Research. 117(D11): D11106. doi:10.1029/2012JD017499. [Date accessed: June 7, 2012].

Lloyd, J.; Farquhar, G.D. 2008. Effects of rising temperatures and CO_2 on the physiology of tropical forest trees. Philosophical Transactions of the Royal Society of London, Series B: Biological Sciences. 363(1498): 1811.

Loescher, H.W.; Oberbauer, S.F; Gholz, H.L.; Clark, D.B. 2003. Environmental controls of net ecosystem-level carbon exchange and productivity in a Central American tropical wet forest. Global Change Biology. 9: 396-412.

Logan, J.A.; Regniere, J.; Powell, J.A. 2003. Assessing the impacts of global warming on forest pest dynamics. Frontiers in Ecology and the Environment. 1(3): 130-137.

Longo, A.V.; Burrowes, P.A.; Joglar, R.L. 2010. Seasonality of *Batrachochytrium dendrobatidis* infection in direct-developing frogs suggests a mechanism for persistence. Diseases of Aquatic Organisms. 92: 253-260.

Lugo, A.E. 2000. Effects and outcomes of Caribbean hurricanes in a climate change scenario. Science of the Total Environment. 262(3): 243-251.

Lugo, A.E.; Brown, S.L.; Dodson, R. [and others]. 1999. The Holdridge life zones of the conterminous United States in relation to ecosystem mapping. Journal of Biogeography. 26(5): 1025-1038.

Lugo, A.E.; Carlo, T.A.; Wunderle, J.M. 2012. Natural mixing of species: novel plant–animal communities on Caribbean islands. Animal Conservation. 15(3): 233-241.

Magrin, G.; Gay García, C.; Cruz Choque, D. [and others]. 2007. Latin America. In: Parry, M.L.; Canziani, O.F.; Palutikof, J.P., comps., eds. Climate Change 2007: Impacts, Adaptation and Vulnerability. Contribution of Working Group II to the Fourth Assessment Report of the Intergovernmental Panel on Climate Change. Cambridge, UK: Cambridge University Press: 581-615.

Malmgren, B.A.; Winter, A.; Chen, D. 1998. El Niño–Southern Oscillation and North Atlantic Oscillation control of climate in Puerto Rico. Journal of Climate. 11(10): 2713-2717.

Marín-Spiotta, E.; Silver, W.L.; Ostertag, R. 2007. Long-term patterns in tropical reforestation: plant community composition and aboveground biomass accumulation. Ecological Applications. 17(3): 828-839.

Martín González, A.M.; Dalsgaard, B.; Ollerton, J. [and others]. 2009. Effects of climate on pollination networks in the West Indies. Journal of Tropical Ecology. 25(05): 493-506.

Martin, H.C.; Weech, P.S. 2001. Climate change in the Bahamas? Evidence in the meteorological records. Bahamas Journal of Science. 8(2): 22–32.

Mazzarella, A.; Scafetta, N. 2012. Evidences for a quasi 60-year North Atlantic Oscillation since 1700 and its meaning for global climate change. Theoretical and Applied Climatology. 107(3): 599-609.

McDowell, N.G.; Beerling, D.J.; Breshears, D.D. [and others]. 2011. The interdependence of mechanisms underlying climate-driven vegetation mortality. Trends in Ecology and Evolution. 26(10): 523-32.

McGroddy, M.; Silver, W.L. 2000. Variations in belowground carbon storage and soil CO_2 flux rates along a wet tropical climate gradient. Biotropica. 32(4a): 614-624.

McKane, R.B ; Rastetter, E.B.; Melillo, J.M. [and others]. 1995. Effects of global change on carbon storage in tropical forests of South America. Global Biogeochemical Cycles. 9(3): 329-350.

Meehl, G.A., Covey, C.; Delworth, T. [and others]. 2007. The WCRP CMIP3 multi-model dataset: a new era in climate change research. Bulletin of the American Meteorological Society. 88: 1383-1394.

Meir, P.; Grace, J.; Miranda, A.C. 2001. Leaf respiration in two tropical rainforests: constraints on physiology by phosphorus, nitrogen and temperature. Functional Ecology. 15(3): 378-387.

Melillo, J. M ; McGuire, A.D.; Kicklighter, D.W. [and others]. 1993. Global climate change and terrestrial net primary production. Nature. 363(6426): 234-240.

Merola-Zwartjes, M.; Ligon, J.D. 2000. Ecological energetics of the Puerto Rican tody: heterothermy, torpor, and intra-island variation. Ecology. 81: 990-1003.

Miles, L.; Grainger, A.; Phillips, O. 2004. The impact of global climate change on tropical forest diversity in Amazonia. Global Ecology and Biogeography. 13: 553-565.

Miller, G.L.; and Lugo, A.E. 2009. Guide to the ecological systems of Puerto Rico. Gen. Tech. Rep. IITF-GTR-35. Rio Piedras, Puerto Rico: U.S. Department of Agriculture Forest Service, International Institute of Tropical Forestry: 436 p.

Mohan, J.E.; Cox, R.M.; Iverson, L.R. 2009. Composition and carbon dynamics of forests in northeastern North America in a future, warmer world. Canadian Journal of Forest Research. 39: 213-230.

Mulholland, P.J ; Best, G.R.; Coutant, C.C. [and others]. 1997. Effects of climate change on freshwater ecosystems of the south-eastern United States and the Gulf Coast of Mexico. Hydrological Processes. 11: 949-970.

Nadkarni, N.; Solano, R. 2002. Potential effects of climate change on canopy communities in a tropical cloud forest: an experimental approach. Oecologia. 131(4): 580-586.

National Oceanic and Atmospheric Administration (NOAA). 2013. Mean sea level trend: 9755371 San Juan, Puerto Rico. Center for Operational Oceanographic Products and Services. http://tidesandcurrents.noaa.gov/sltrends/sltrends_station.shtml?stnid=9755371 [Date accessed: September 20, 2013].

Neelin, J.D.; Münnich, M.; Su, H. [and others]. 2006. Tropical drying trends in global warming models and observations. Proceedings of the National Academy of Sciences. 103(16): 6110-6115.

Nicholson, K.L.; Torrence, S.M ; Ghioca, D.M. [and others]. 2005. The influence of temperature and humidity on activity patterns of the lizards *Anolis stratulus* and *Ameiva exsul* in the British Virgin Islands. Caribbean Journal of Science. 41(4): 870-873.

O'Brien, S.T ; Hayden, B.P.; Shugart, H.H. 1992. Global climatic change, hurricanes, and a tropical forest. Climatic Change. 22: 175-190.

Olaya-Arenas, P ; Meléndez-Ackerman, E.J.; Pérez, M.E.; Tremblay, R. 2011. Demographic response by a small epiphytic orchid. American Journal of Botany. 98(12): 2040-2048.

Oliveira, R.S ; Dawson, T.E.; Burgess, S.S.; Nepstad, D.C. 2005. Hydraulic redistribution in three Amazonian trees. Oecologia. 145(3): 354-363.

Ortiz-Zayas, J.R.; Cuevas, E.; Mayol-Bracero, O.L. [and others]. 2006. Urban influences on the nitrogen cycle in Puerto Rico. Biogeochemistry. 79(1-2): 109-133.

Ospina, O.E.; Villanueva-Rivera, L.J.; Corrada-Bravo, C.J ; Aide, T.M. 2013. Variable response of anuran calling activity to daily precipitation and temperature: implications for climate change. Ecosphere. 4(4): article 47.

Pardow, A.; Lakatos, M. 2013. Desiccation tolerance and global change: implications for tropical bryophytes in lowland forests. Biotropica. 45(1): 27-36.

Parris, A.; Bromirski, P.; Burkett, V. [and others]. 2012. Global sea level rise scenarios for the U.S. National Climate Assessment. NOAA Tech. Memo. OAR-CPO-1. Silver Springs, MD: National Oceanic and Atmospheric Administration, Climate Program Office. 37 p.

Patiño-Martínez, J.; Marco, A.; Quiñones, L.; Hawkes, L. 2012. A potential tool to mitigate the impacts of climate change to the Caribbean leatherback sea turtle. Global Change Biology. 18(2): 401-411.

Pau, S.; Wolkovich, E.M.; Cook, B.I. [and others]. 2011. Predicting phenology by integrating ecology, evolution and climate science. Global Change Biology. 17: 3633-3643.

Perry, G.; Dmi'el, R.; Lazell, J. 2000. Evaporative water loss in insular populations of *Anolis cristatellus* (Reptilia: Sauria) in the British Virgin Islands. III. Response to the end of drought and a common garden experiment. Biotropica. 32 (4a): 722-728.

Peterson, T.C.; Taylor, M.A.; Demeritte, R. [and others]. 2002. Recent changes in climate extremes in the Caribbean region. Journal of Geophysical Research. 107(D21): 4601.

Phillips, O.L.; Baker, T.R.; Arroyo, L. [and others]. 2004. Pattern and process in Amazon tree turnover, 1976–2001. Philosophical Transactions of the Royal Society of London, Series B: Biological Sciences. 359(1443): 381-407.

Phillips, O.L.; Gentry, A.H. 1994. Increasing turnover through time in tropical forests. Science. 263: 954–958.

Pickles, B.J.; Egger, K.N.; Massicotte, H.B.; Green, D.S. 2012. Ectomycorrhizas and climate change. Fungal Ecology. 5(1): 73-84.

Ping, C-L.; Michaelson, G.J.; Stiles, C.A.; González, G. 2013. Soil characteristics, carbon stores, and nutrient distribution in eight forest types along an elevation gradient, eastern Puerto Rico. Ecological Bulletins. 54: 67–86.

Pounds, J.A.; Fogden, M.P.L.; Campbell, J.H. 1999. Biological response to climate change on a tropical mountain. Nature. 398(6728): 611-615.

Presley, S.J.; Willig, M.R.; Bloch, C.P. [and others]. 2011. A complex metacommunity structure for gastropods along an elevational gradient. Biotropica. 43(4): 480-488.

Prideaux, B.; Coghlan, A.; McNamara, K. 2010. Assessing tourists' perceptions of climate change on mountain landscapes. Tourism Recreation Research. 35(2): 187-199.

Pringle, C.M.; Scatena, F.N. 1999. Aquatic ecosystem deterioration in Latin America and the Caribbean. In: Hatch, L.J.; Swisher, M. E.; eds. Managed ecosystems: the Mesoamerican experience. New York: Oxford University Press: 292 p.

Prospero, J.M.; Lamb, P.J. 2003. African droughts and dust transport to the Caribbean: climate change implications. Science. 302(5647): 1024-1027.

Puerto Rico Climate Change Council (PRCCC). 2013. State of Puerto Rico's climate 2010–2013 executive summary. Assessing Puerto Rico's social-ecological vulnerabilities in a changing climate. San Juan, PR: Puerto Rico Coastal Zone Management Program, Department of Natural and Environmental Resources, Office of Ocean and Coastal Resource Management (NOAA-OCRM): 27 p. http://www.drna.gobierno.pr/oficinas/arn/recursosvivientes/costasreservasrefugios/pmzc/prccc/prccc-2013/PRCCC_ExecutiveSummary_ElectronicVersion_English.pdf. [Date accessed: November 4, 2013].

Quiñones, M.; Rivera, L; Gould, W. 2013. El Yunque National Forest vegetation map. Appears in terrestrial ecosystem assessment chapter of the land and resources management plan revision for El Yunque National Forest. Vector data. U.S. Department of Agriculture Forest Service. San Juan, PR.

Raich, J.W.; Russell, A.E.; Kitayama, K. [and others]. 2006. Temperature influences carbon accumulation in moist tropical forests. Ecology. 87: 76-87.

Rivera-Ocasio, E.; Aide, T.M.; Rios-Lopez, N. 2007. The effects of salinity on the dynamics of a *Pterocarpus officinalis* forest stand in Puerto Rico. Journal of Tropical Ecology. 23: 559-568.

Robbins, A.M; Eckelmann, C.M.; Quiñones, M. 2008. Forest fires in the insular Caribbean. AMBIO: A Journal of the Human Environment. 37(7): 528-534.

Rodenhouse, N.L.; Matthews, S.N.; McFarland, K.P. [and others]. 2008. Potential effects of climate change on birds of the Northeast. Mitigation and Adaptation Strategies for Global Change. 13(5-6): 517-540.

Rogowitz, G.L. 1996. Evaluation of thermal acclimation and altitudinal variation of metabolism in a neotropical lizard, *Anolis gundlachi*. Copeia. 1996(3): 535.

Royo, A.A.; Scalley, T.H.; Moya, S.; Scatena, F.N. 2011. Non-arborescent vegetation trajectories following repeated hurricane disturbance: ephemeral versus enduring responses. Ecosphere. 2(7): 1-17.

Scatena, F.N. 1998. An assessment of climate change in the Luquillo Mountains of Puerto Rico. In: Segarra-García, R.I., ed. Proceeding tropical hydrology and Caribbean water resources, Third International Symposium on Tropical Hydrology and Fifth Caribbean Islands Water Resources Congress in San Juan, Puerto Rico. Herndon, VA: American Water Resources Association: 193-198.

Scatena, F.N.; Lugo A.E. 1998. Geomorphology, disturbance, and the soil and vegetation of two subtropical wet steepland watersheds of Puerto Rico. Geomorphology. 13(4): 199-213.

Schellekens, J.; Scatena, F. N ; Bruijnzeel, L.A. [and others]. 2004. Stormflow generation in a small rainforest catchment in the Luquillo Experimental Forest, Puerto Rico. Hydrological Processes. 18(3): 505-530.

Scott, D ; McBoyle, G.; Schwartzentruber, M. 2004. Climate change and the distribution of climatic resources for tourism in North America. Climate Research. 27(2): 105-117.

Scott, D ; Simpson, M.C ; Sim, R. 2012. The vulnerability of Caribbean coastal tourism to scenarios of climate change related sea level rise. Journal of Sustainable Tourism. 20(6): 883-898.

Seager, R.; Tzanova, A.; Nakamura, J. 2009. Drought in the south-eastern United States: causes, variability over the last millennium, and the potential for future hydroclimate change. American Meteorological Society. 22(19): 5021-5045.

Seavy, N.E.; Gardali, T.; Golet, G.H. [and others]. 2009. Why climate change makes riparian restoration more important than ever: recommendations for practice and research. Ecological Restoration. 27(3): 330-338.

Şekercioğlu, Ç.H ; Primack, R. B.; Wormworth, J. 2012. The effects of climate change on tropical birds. Biological Conservation. 148(1): 1-18.

Şekercioğlu, Ç.H ; Schneider, S.H.; Fay, J.P; Loarie, S.R. 2008. Climate change, elevational range shifts, and bird extinctions. Conservation Biology. 22: 140-150.

Seneviratne, S.I.; Nicholls, N.; Easterling, D. [and others]. 2012. Changes in climate extremes and their impacts on the natural physical environment. In: Field, C.B. [and others], eds. Managing the Risks of Extreme Events and Disasters to Advance Climate Change Adaptation. A Special Report of Working Groups I and II of the Intergovernmental Panel on Climate Change (IPCC). Cambridge, UK, and New York: Cambridge University Press: 109-230.

Shanley, J.B.; Mast, M.A.; Campbell, D.H. [and others]. 2008. Comparison of total mercury and methylmercury cycling at five sites using the small watershed approach. Environmental Pollution. 154(1): 143-154.

Sherman, R.E ; Martin, P.H.; Fahey, T.J.; Degloria, S.D. 2008. Fire and vegetation dynamics in high-elevation neotropical montane forests of the Dominican Republic. AMBIO: A Journal of the Human Environment. 37(7): 535-541.

Silver, W.L. 1998. The potential effects of elevated CO_2 and climate change on tropical forest soils and biogeochemical cycling. Climatic Change. 39: 337-361.

Silver, W.L.; Kueppers, L.M ; Lugo, A.E. [and others]. 2004. Carbon sequestration and plant community dynamics following reforestation of tropical pasture. Ecological Applications. 14(4): 1115-1127.

Silver, W.L.; Lugo, A.E.; Keller, M. 1999. Soil oxygen availability and biogeochemistry along rainfall and topographic gradients in upland wet tropical forest soils. Biogeochemistry. 44(3): 301-328.

Smith, J.A.M.; Reitsma, L.R.; Marra, P.P. 2010. Moisture as a determinant of habitat quality for a nonbreeding neotropical migratory songbird. Ecology. 91(10): 2874-2882.

Stallard, R.F. 2001. Possible environmental factors underlying amphibian decline in eastern Puerto Rico: analysis of U.S. government data archives. Conservation Biology. 15(4): 943-953.

Stewart, M.M. 1995. Climate driven population fluctuations in rain forest frogs. Journal of Herpetology. 28: 369-378.

Still, C.J.; Foster, P.N.; Schneider, S.H. 1999. Simulating the effects of climate change on tropical montane cloud forests. Nature. 398(6728): 608-610.

Stork, N.E.; Balston, J ; Farquhar, G.D. [and others]. 2007. Tropical rainforest canopies and climate change. Austral Ecology. 32(1): 105-112.

Stork, N.E.; Coddington, J.A.; Colwell, R.K. [and others]. 2009. Vulnerability and resilience of tropical forest species to land-use change. Conservation Biology. 23(6): 1438-1447.

Studds, C.E.; Marra, P.P. 2011. Rainfall-induced changes in food availability modify the spring departure programme of a migratory bird. Proceedings of the Royal Society of London, Series B: Biological Sciences. 278(1723): 3437-3443.

Sturrock, R.N.; Frankel, S.J ; Brown, A.V. [and others]. 2011. Climate change and forest diseases. Plant Pathology. 60: 133-149.

Tewksbury, J.J.; Huey, R.B.; Deutsch, C.A. 2008. Putting the heat on tropical animals. Science. 320(5881): 1296-1297.

Thompson, J.; Lugo, A.E.; Thomlinson, J. 2007. Land use history, hurricane disturbance, and the fate of introduced species in a subtropical wet forest in Puerto Rico. Plant Ecology. 192(2): 289-301.

Tian, H.; Melillo, J.M.; Kicklighter, D.W. [and others]. 1998. Effect of interannual climate variability on carbon storage in Amazonian ecosystems. Nature. 396(6712): 664-667.

Toms, J.D.; Faaborg, J.; Arendt, W.J. 2012. Climate change and birds in the forgotten tropics: the importance of tropical dry forests. Ibis. 154(3): 632-634.

Torres, I.; González, J.E.; Comarazamy, D.E. 2008. Impacts of a changing climate and low land use on a tropical montane cloud forest. Environmental Problems in Coastal Regions VII. 99: 60-70.

Tran, D.B.; Dargusch, P.; Moss, P.; Hoang, T.V. 2012. An assessment of potential responses of *Melaleuca* genus to global climate change. Mitigation and Adaptation Strategies for Global Change. 18(6): 851-867.

Treasure, E.; McNulty, S.; Moore Myers, J.; Jennings, L.N. 2014. Template for Assessing Climate Change Impacts and Management Options: user guide (Version 2.2). Gen. Tech. Rep. SRS-186. Asheville, NC: U.S. Department of Agriculture Forest Service, Southern Research Station. 33 p.

U.S. Department of Agriculture (USDA) Forest Service. 2012. National Forest System Land Management Planning (Final rule and record of decision). Federal Register 77:68 (April 9, 2012): 21162 p. http://www.fs.usda.gov/Internet/FSE_DOCUMENTS/stelprdb5362536.pdf. [Date accessed: April 10, 2012].

Uriarte, M.; Yackulic, C.B.; Lim, Y.; Arce-Nazario, J.A. 2011. Influence of land use on water quality in a tropical landscape: a multi-scale analysis. Landscape Ecology. 26(8): 1151-1164.

Uyarra, M.C.; Côté, I.M.; Gill, J.A. [and others]. 2005. Island-specific preferences of tourists for environmental features: implications of climate change for tourism-dependent states. Environmental Conservation. 32(1): 11-19.

Van der Molen, M.K.; Vugts, H.F.; Bruijnzeel, L.A. [and others]. 2010. Meso-scale climate change due to lowland deforestation in the maritime tropics. In: Bruijnzeel, L.A.; Scatena, F.N.; Hamilton, L.S., eds. Tropical Montane Cloud Forests: Science for Conservation and Management. New York: Cambridge University Press: 527-537. http://www.cambridge.org/9780521760355. [Date accessed: June 18, 2013].

Van Mantgem, P.J.; Stephenson, N.L.; Byrne, J.C. [and others]. 2009. Widespread increase of tree mortality rates in the western United States. Science. 323(5913): 521-524.

Vélez Rodríguez, Z.; Votaw, G.S. 2012. Precipitation in Puerto Rico and U.S. Virgin Islands. National Oceanic and Atmospheric Administration, San Juan, PR. 6 p. http://www.srh.noaa.gov/Image s/sju/climo/GV2012.pdf [Date accessed: August 22, 2013].

Wagner, F.; Rossi, V.; Stahl, C. [and others]. 2012. Water availability is the main climate driver of neotropical tree growth. PLoS ONE. 7(4): e34074. http://dx.plos.org/10 1371/journal.pone.0034074. [Date accessed: June 18, 2013].

Waide, R.B.; Comarazamy, D.E.; González, J.E. [and others]. 2013. Climate variability at multiple spatial and temporal scales in the Luquillo Mountains, Puerto Rico. Ecological Bulletins. 54: 21-41.

Walther, G.R.; Post, E.; Convey, P. [and others]. 2002. Ecological responses to recent climate change. Nature. 416(6879): 389-395.

Wang, H.; Cornell, J.D.; Hall, C.A.S.; Marley, D.P. 2002. Spatial and seasonal dynamics of surface soil carbon in the Luquillo Experimental Forest, Puerto Rico. Ecological Modelling. 147(2): 105-122.

Wang, H.; Hall, C.A.S.; Scatena, F.N. [and others]. 2003. Modeling the spatial and temporal variability in climate and primary productivity across the Luquillo Mountains, Puerto Rico. Forest Ecology and Management. 179(1): 69-94.

Wang, Y.P.; Houlton, B.Z. 2009. Nitrogen constraints on terrestrial carbon uptake: implications for the global carbon-climate feedback. Geophysical Research Letters. 36(24): L24403. doi:10 1029/2009GL041009. [Date accessed: October 10, 2012].

Wardle, D.A.; Williamson, W.M.; Yeates, G.W.; Bonner, K.I. 2005. Trickle-down effects of aboveground trophic cascades on the soil food web. Oikos. 111(2): 348-358.

Way, D.A.; Oren, R. 2010. Differential responses to changes in growth temperature between trees from different functional groups and biomes: a review and synthesis of data. Tree Physiology. 30(6): 669-688.

Weaver, P.L. 2012. The Luquillo Mountains: forest resources and their history. Gen. Tech. Rep. IITF-GTR-44. Rio Piedras, Puerto Rico: U.S. Department of Agriculture Forest Service, International Institute of Tropical Forestry: 159 p.

Werth, D.; Avissar, R. 2002. The local and global effects of Amazon deforestation. Journal of Geophysical Research. 107(D20): 8087.

White, A.; Cannell, M.G.R.; Friend, A.D. 2000. CO_2 stabilization, climate change and the terrestrial carbon sink. Global Change Biology. 6(7): 817-833.

Whitmore, T.C. 1998. Potential impact of climatic change on tropical rain forest seedlings and forest regeneration. Climatic Change. 39(2-3): 429-438.

Wood, T.E.; Cavaleri, M.A.; Reed, S.C. 2012. Tropical forest carbon balance in a warmer world: a critical review spanning microbial-to ecosystem-scale processes. Biological Reviews. 87(4): 912-927.

Wood, T.E.; Lawrence, D.; Clark, D.A.; Chazdon, R.L. 2009. Rain forest nutrient cycling and productivity in response to large-scale litter manipulation. Ecology. 90(1): 109-121.

Wood, T.E.; Silver, W.L. 2012. Strong spatial variability in trace gas dynamics following experimental drought in a humid tropical forest. Global Biogeochemical Cycles. 26(3): GB3005.

Woollings, T.; Blackburn, M. 2012. The North Atlantic Jet Stream under climate change and its relation to the NAO and EA Patterns. Journal of Climate. 25(3): 886-902.

Wu, W.; Hall, C.; Zhang, L. 2006. Predicting the temporal and spatial probability of orographic cloud cover in the Luquillo Experimental Forest in Puerto Rico using generalized linear (mixed) models. Ecological Modelling. 192(3-4): 473-498.

Wunderle, J.M.; Arendt, W.J. 2011. Avian studies and research opportunities in the Luquillo Experimental Forest: a tropical rain forest in Puerto Rico. Forest Ecology and Management. 262(1): 33-48.

Yeh, S.-W.; Kug, J.-S.; Dewitte, B. [and others]. 2009. El Niño in a changing climate. Nature. 461(7263): 511-514.

Yeh, S.-W.; Park, Y.-G; Kirtman, B.P. 2006. ENSO amplitude changes in climate change commitment to atmospheric CO_2 doubling. Geophysical Research Letters. 33:13 [Not paged]. doi:10.1029/2005GL025653. [Date accessed: June 6, 2012].

Zhou, X.; Fu, Y.; Zhou, L. [and others]. 2013. An imperative need for global change research in tropical forests. Tree Physiology. 33(9): 903-912.

Zotz, G.; Bader, M.Y. 2009. Epiphytic plants in a changing world-global: change effects on vascular and non-vascular epiphytes. In: Lüttge, U.; Beyschlag, W.; Büdel, B., comps. eds. Progress in Botany. Vol. 70(4). Berlin, Heidelberg: Springer-Verlag: 147-170.

Appendix: Science Summary Methodology

Information presented in this appendix provides a summary of methods and an example of translating the Template for Assessing Climate Change Impacts and Management Options (TACCIMO) direct output—in the form of annotated bibliography-style quotations—to scientific summaries in order to aid in the understanding of information sources and to provide guidance for science delivery. The use of TACCIMO within the context of the 2012 *Planning Rule* (USDA Forest Service 2012) allows forest planners and managers to identify best available sources of information quickly and consistently. TACCIMO provides users with an interactive framework that efficiently delivers climate change science needed to assess, manage, and monitor forest resources under a changing climate. The inclusion of information in TACCIMO is performed following documented methods and criteria designed to ensure scientific integrity (Treasure and others 2014). This information reflects an extensive literature review process concentrating on the effects of climate change on key physical, ecological, and social resources within the geographic areas of interest. TACCIMO's public facing website (www.forestthreats.org/taccimotool) provides a standardized and scalable resource to help meet the needs of planners and managers throughout the United States and greater Caribbean region. Literature-based science is organized into a dynamic and interactive information framework that allows for rapid addition of new and emerging science and efficient access to a wide variety of subject matter. Planning efforts in El Yunque National Forest (EYNF) under the 2012 *Planning Rule* provide an ideal venue to apply extensive content development as reflected in this report, which goes beyond the base level of support afforded to all Forest Service regions.

Best available climate change science selected for addition to the TACCIMO database undergoes a traditional literature review process in which key sections of the paper are highlighted for further analysis. The highlighted information is then subject to an organizational framework where quotations are categorized based on key themes. Quotes, rather than paraphrases, are preserved to reduce subjectivity and allow for literal linkages back to primary sources and supporting literature. Careful consideration is given to the context from which quotations are taken, but quotation by its very nature requires application of judgment and results in loss of context. To abate the loss of context to the greatest extent possible, and to promote the highest level of data quality in TACCIMO, the following criteria are strictly applied:

- Literature is peer reviewed, either as stated by the publishing journal's guidelines, explicitly within the paper, or by personal contact with the author.
- The subject and theme of the quotation are consistent with the subject and theme of the source as a whole.
- The conclusion of the selected quotation is clearly substantiated by the scientific evidence reported in the source article and cited supporting literature.
- If the claim is synthesis-based, supporting literature citations substantiate the synthesized conclusion.
- The length of the quotation is kept to the minimum length sufficient for understanding the statement independent of accompanying text.
- Qualifying statements and statements addressing uncertainty are included.

Information in TACCIMO can be easily consumed through exploring and reporting tools, allowing natural resource professionals to quickly identify credible sources of climate change information. Once key sources are identified, quotations within a category can be translated into scientific summaries to capture key concepts. To maintain the quality of the scientific information, summaries should contain information regarding (1) the area or region of study, (2) the time period of observational and empirical data, (3) the affected species or experimental unit, and (4) stated uncertainties and limitations, when available.

All summaries should contain citations back to the original source and any secondary sources and should reference only information cited by or hypothesized by the authors (e.g., no added statements such as "there will likely be" or "probably").

The following scientific summaries and TACCIMO outputs for historic temperature trends are provided as an example of this process. Scientific summaries are excerpted directly from the text of this document. Below the summaries, direct TACCIMO quotations are provided, taken directly from the TACCIMO database. For a comprehensive list of direct quotations describing the effects of climate change on resources in Puerto Rico and the greater Caribbean region, see the TACCIMO Geographic Region Explorer for the Caribbean (online at http://www.taccimo.sgcp ncsu.edu/DirectImpactRegionContent. aspx?RegionID=19).

Example 1

- In the tropical montane cloud forest at Pico del Este in EYNF, mean monthly minimum temperatures have increased over the past 30 years (Lasso and Ackerman 2003). Similar changes were also found in the Monteverde Cloud Forest Reserve in Costa Rica, where temperatures have increased about 2 °C (LaVal 2004, Pounds and others 1999).

Lasso, E.; Ackerman, J.D. 2003. Flowering phenology of *Werauhia sintenisii*, a bromeliad from the dwarf montane forest in Puerto Rico: an indicator of climate change? Selbyana. 24(1): 95-104.
"At Pico del Este, a TMCF [tropical montane cloud forest] in Puerto Rico, environmental conditions have changed during the last 30 years. Monthly mean minimum temperature has increased along with a trend for more days with ≥ 12.7 mm precipitation (FIGURE 1)."

LaVal, R.K. 2004. Impact of global warming and locally changing climate on tropical cloud forest bats. Journal of Mammalogy. 85(2): 237-244.
"Because climatological data from the early 1970s to the present are available, Pounds and his coauthors were able to correlate changes in weather patterns with distribution and abundance of amphibians, reptiles, and birds, including species extinctions (Pounds et al. 1999). From these climatic data, Pounds et al. (1999) found that the frequency of MCF [Monteverde Cloud Forest Reserve] dry season mist had decreased, average altitude at the base of the orographic cloud bank had risen, and mean minimum temperatures have in-creased about 2 C during this period."

Example 2

- Mean annual temperatures in the Caribbean have increased an average of 0.2 to 0.4 °C each decade since 1976 (IPCC 2001, Uyarra and others 2005). Average overnight low and daytime high temperatures have also increased in the Caribbean by 1.0 and 1.8 °C, respectively, since 1950 (Comarazamy and González 2011).

Uyarra, M.C.; Côté, I.M.; Gill, J.A. [and others]. 2005. Island-specific preferences of tourists for environmental features: implications of climate change for tourism-dependent states. Environmental Conservation. 32(1): 11-19.
"Mean atmospheric temperature in the eastern Caribbean has increased by 0.2– 0.4 C per decade since 1976, and recent models indicate that it might rise by 1.4–5.8 C in the next century (IPCC [Intergovernmental Panel on Climate Change] 2001)."

Comarazamy, D.E.; González, J.E. 2011. Regional long-term climate change (1950–2000) in the midtropical Atlantic and its impacts on the hydrological cycle of Puerto Rico. Journal of Geophysical Research. 116(D21): D00Q05.
"The large-scale temperature changes at the times of local overnight low and daytime high temperatures over the Caribbean region show moderate increases in temperature [in the early rainfall season (April-June) for the 1950-2000 time frame] on the order of 1.0 to 1.8 C, respectively; these values increase toward the North Atlantic."

Jennings, L.N.; Douglas, J.; Treasure, E.; and González, G. 2014. Climate change effects in El Yunque National Forest, Puerto Rico, and the Caribbean region. Gen. Tech. Rep. SRS-193. Asheville, NC: U.S. Department of Agriculture Forest Service, Southern Research Station. 47 p.

Understanding the current and expected future conditions of natural resources under a changing climate is essential to making informed management decisions. However, the ever-increasing volume of useful scientific information about climate change makes it difficult for managers and planners to effectively sort through and apply the emerging science. This report provides a knowledge base of peer-reviewed climate change science for El Yunque National Forest (also administratively designated as the Luquillo Experimental Forest), Puerto Rico, and the greater Caribbean region. We summarized scientific findings from over 240 peer-reviewed sources, covering a wide range of potential effects including changes to drivers and stressors and the effects of climate change on ecological, physical, social, and economic systems. Projected and observed changes include increases in air temperatures, an extension of the dry season, and changes in cloud cover that may lead to significant alterations to the diverse plant and animal communities of the Caribbean region. Species in cloud forests on isolated mountain peaks may be most at risk, due to sensitivities to moisture and a limited chance for migration. Changes in extreme weather patterns, including an increase in hurricane intensity and more frequent drought events, are projected to alter the distribution of tropical forest vegetation. Tourism patterns and recreational opportunities may change with an increase in extreme weather and impacts from sea level rise. The information presented in this report provides a starting point for natural resource managers, planners, and stakeholders to assess the vulnerability of local resources to climate change as part of a broader decision-making framework.

Keywords: Assessment, Caribbean, climate change, El Yunque National Forest, forest planning, Luquillo Experimental Forest, technology transfer.

 **How do you rate this publication?**

Scan this code to submit your feedback or go to www.srs.fs.usda.gov/pubeval